THE AMERICAN DOCTOR

Hi Mark

Enjoy the book and
Pass on the inspiration
John Adah 10/31/18

THE AMERICAN DOCTOR

The Boy from an African Village

DR. JOHN ACQUAYE-AWAH

ISBN-13: 9780692055328
ISBN-10: 0692055320
Library of Congress Control Number: 2018900445
American Doctor, The, Chicago, IL

CONTENTS

DEDICATION

This book is dedicated to my parents, Emmanuel Kwadjo Awah and Karley Acquaye- Awah. I am grateful for the confidence they had in me and for providing me with all the tools I needed to survive. They did not live long enough to enjoy the fruit of their labor. I wish to cherish their memories for as long as humanity exists.

INTRODUCTION

This book depicts how a young boy from the remotest village in Africa was able to beat all the odds to become an established doctor in the United States of America. A few people who share my background have made similar journeys, but their stories remain untold. Having come across many people in my adulthood who lament over little bumps in their lives as excuses and impediments to their success, I feel I have to narrate the extremes others have to go through in order to be successful.

This book walks you through the life of a typical village boy who was born to illiterate parents in a village where there was no running water or electricity and who was secluded from the outside world by a lack of television and the World Wide Web. A life where walking barefoot across rough terrains for miles in order to attend school was the norm of the day.

Recognizing at an early age that the shortened life expectancy in the village was because of a combination of extreme poverty, bad cultural beliefs, and ancient medical practices, my choice to become a doctor to help improve this was not difficult to make.

However, while embarking on this journey, I had to navigate all the odd nuances entrenched in the village so that I did not become one of the statistics of abrogated life expectancy.

My journey has also been complicated by my extreme passion in business, which I pursued alongside my quest to become a doctor. I soon realized that unlike the academic path, which was well structured, my business journey was like a whirlwind that floored me many times. However, I was able to weather the storm and used the mistakes to improve my course.

As I popped out of the bubble of my secluded world in the village in pursuit of my dream, I quickly discovered that the rest of the world was full of varied cultural differences that were alien to mine. To fit in, I had to adapt and accept the differences. Today, this has prepared me in my career to deal with a wide range of people from all walks of life.

Having experienced raw poverty firsthand, I know how it feels when I find someone in that situation. Today, I feel heartbroken to see people go through what I experienced. I always feel obliged to help everyone in need so they do not have to go through the same hardship. This has propelled me to give back to society where it is appropriate. As a result, I have contributed in lightening the load of many deprived people, including my family and total strangers.

The small village I grew up in is called Oterkpolu, and at the time I was born, it had a population of a few hundred. The mud houses that constituted the village were strung along a T-junction linking a major market to two major cities. It had a low life expectancy, which was an effect of low education, lack of health care, and the belief that sickness and death were because of supernatural powers. Most of my childhood friends who were not fortunate enough to make it past basic education remained in the village and died in their primes from simple illnesses.

I was fortunate to be smart in school and have a relatively well-to-do dad. By these virtues, I was given a head start in secondary education, where I was discovered by the education authorities and immediately awarded a government scholarship. Now that a school fee was no longer an issue, I was able to use my academic prowess to successfully climb all the ladders of education. I broke many educational records. I could become whatever I chose to be, and I decided to become a doctor. This was a profession that I felt was perfectly in tune with my character.

Along the way, while I was acquiring an education, I indulged in my other passion: business. I started my business ventures at the age of fifteen. I was immediately exposed to the reality checks of the world of business. Anything could go wrong with what appeared to be an easy moneymaker. My successes in business were equally matched by failures. However, my failures did not stop my keenness in business, but rather, I capitalized on them to do better. The net effect was that I became a successful businessman. I was attuned to looking at setbacks as opportunities rather than failures. Right before I completed medical school, I became the first person in Ghana to set up a medical supplies shop. This was a niche market I accidentally discovered, and it rapidly grew overnight. This was the first time I made a significant profit in business.

Throughout my formative years, I was faced with many misfortunes. But somehow these misfortunes turned out to be a blessing. It was as if had the misfortune not happened, the good end result would not have become a reality. This consistency became so glaring that it defined my perception of apparent problems in life and toughened me up.

After my basic medical training in Ghana, I went to England for further education and then to the United States. I finally settled in Chicago. I combined my profession and my business acumen in my work in Chicago. This resulted in a very successful and prosperous medical business. With my potential evident, I was selected as a member of the board of directors of Michael Reese Hospital in Chicago.

I invested the fortunes I made from my medical practice in Chicago in Ghana. I am now aspiring to be a successful hotelier and fish farmer there.

My third passion, philanthropy, is exemplified by my being able to raise money to help Vincent. He had a brain tumor in Ghana, where they did not have the expertise to treat him. He was recommended to go to India for treatment. All attempts by him to raise money for his treatment failed. He was left on a deadly course. I came across him by chance or by divine design. I immediately rallied my close friends in the United States and raised the money for his treatment. I was then able to sponsor him to go to India for a successful surgery. Vincent was so grateful that soon after he returned home, he went to the high court of Ghana and added my last name to his. His official name is now Vincent Woode Awah.

Perhaps what matters most in life is where one is going rather than where one comes from. You can become whatever you want if you have a vision and the will. Only you can make a difference in your life. This chronicle exemplifies what many successful persons have been through. There will be many bumps in the road, but these must not be used as excuses preventing one's success.

Chapter 1

OTERKPOLU

My journey began in Oterkpolu in March 1960. There I took my first breath of life—a life full of hope and vigor, which started in a village that is tucked away in the valleys of the eastern corner of Ghana. The valleys were where many of my contemporaries succumbed to simple ailments like common colds that became complicated because of lack of treatment. It was a challenging environment where survival depended on the human body's own natural resilience. Maneuvering myself from these challenging valleys and emerging unscathed convinced me that I was selected for a purpose, a natural selection that had been proven by Darwin: the survival of the fittest. The surviving genes have been propagated and passed on to my progeny. This I can see in my children today in America. They are chalking life's expected milestones with ease; little do they know that they are products of a good genetic selection.

Come with me to visit this village called Oterkpolu, a village full of superstitious beliefs. Every misfortune was promptly attributed to imaginary spirits. No one died a natural death. Death was always because of someone else's doings, either through juju or witchcraft.

The belief in witchcraft was heavily entrenched. The grandmothers or the oldest females in some families were usually accused of being witches—and a lot of times to their detriment. They were jeered and scorned. Some were left neglected and to their demise because of the belief that they may have caused harm to someone.

The juju men were the most powerful. Their shrines were scary. No one wanted to be on the wrong side of a juju man. They were believed to inflict illnesses or death on people. No one had ever proven these claims, and no one dared.

In general, the villagers were very content with their lives or at least appeared to be, shortsighted in their wants, and shielded from the world of material things. They did not miss what they did not know. Their exposure to the polluted world of wants and needs was through the radio, which was limited to relatively affluent homes. My father had one such big radio, which he proudly displayed in his sitting room, covered with the most expensive white lacy material. There was no television, or I should more accurately say that the name did not exist then.

No one wore a wristwatch; simply put, it was luxurious to have one, and no one could afford it. But time was immaterial. My father, a bit more affluent, had a huge pendulum clock whose hourly chimes could be heard in our next-door neighbor's house. Time was measured by the position of the sun. Sunrise was 6:00 a.m., the midday sun was overhead, and sunset was 6:00 p.m. It was equatorial, so they were right. Minutes were measured in eye blinks, and one eye blink was one minute. The cockcrow was used to measure the dawn hours. The first cockcrow was 3:00 a.m., the second was 4:00 a.m., and the third was 5:00 a.m. It was not safe to wake up and be on the roads at the first cockcrow because the witches and ghosts were still roaming. After the third cockcrow was when it was safe to be up and about.

The food was basic. I thought it was poor man's food until I came to the Western world. They call it Whole Foods in the United States. It was full of vegetables and tubers uncontaminated by chemicals and genetic modifications. Fish, free-range chicken, free-range goat, and game were the main sources of protein. People walked everywhere in the village. Is that not the lifestyle the "cool people" in America now strive to live?

Medications were herbal. There were designated herbalists who had a cure for everything. They kept the contents of their concoctions and potions secret, and they died with them. I am sure they had good things to offer, but their knowledge dissipated with their demise and was never passed on.

Oterkpolu is located in the eastern region of Ghana. It is fourteen miles from the nearest regional capital of Koforidua. Situated at a T-junction linking three commercial towns, it was chosen as a strategic location for my father to set up his mechanic business. Its population was under one thousand when I was growing up. Bordering two sides of the village are mountain ranges populated by thick, rich, tropical forest. The village has rich and fertile agricultural land, making subsistence farming a logical and vibrant occupation.

Farming was very tedious manual labor. Most of the villagers were unable to afford to hire labor. The labor fell back on the household. Men, women, and children alike played their part. The bigger the household, the bigger the farm and the bigger the amount of money the household generated.

I started farm labor at the age of five. On school days, we woke up at dawn and spent two to three hours tilling the land. Then we went back home and got ready for school, which started at 8:00 a.m. After school, at 4:00 p.m., we went back to the farm and worked until dark, which set in at about 6:00 p.m. The farms were usually about one to two miles from home, and the only means of transport was walking. This is how we, unknowingly, got our exercise.

The farm produce included vegetables, tubers, and legumes. This fed the house all year round.

Like all parts of Ghana, the village relied on the two rainy seasons to water its crops. Not uncommonly, the rains would fail, and the resultant scanty farm yield caused sporadic famine and malnutrition.

Fish and game were the main sources of protein. The forest was full of wild animals, including antelopes and big rats. These were all killed and eaten to near extinction. A big river called the River Pompon, which is now a shadow of itself as a result of global warming, served as a source of natural fresh fish and crustaceans, including tilapia, catfish, and huge crabs.

There was some sort of barter system whereby, on the two market days, the fishermen and the farmers met to exchange their produce. There was no concept of units, and eyeball equivalents settled the nuances of supply and demand.

Health care was very rudimentary. The choices for ill health were either let-
ting the body heal naturally, visiting the herbalist, or attending the nearest hospital
fourteen miles away if the family could afford it. The common ailments included
infectious diseases like cholera, diarrhea, worm infestation, anemia, malnutrition, and snake bites. Others were measles; polio; and kwashiorkor, a term for
severe protein malnutrition. In later years, HIV and AIDS became rampant.

Paradoxically, there was a mixture of early deaths and survivals Those people who were able to maneuver the harshness of village life without medical
care and dodge the dangers of being afflicted with potentially life-threatening
diseases of childhood and adolescence were either lucky or specially chosen. I
feel I am one of the selected few who were meant to survive and pass on the
enduring genes.

The housing in Oterkpolu was also very basic. It was a conglomeration of
helter-skelter mud structures across a field of agricultural land. With no town
planning in place, the houses were placed very close to one another, making
room for only footpaths. This probably made sense when none of the villagers
could ever in their lifetimes dream of owning a vehicle.

The homes were mostly roofed with thatch. Those with a bit more money
were able to afford aluminum roofing sheets, which clearly stood as a status
symbol. The flooring of the homes was dried mud. Again, the relatively wealthy
households were able to afford polished concrete floors. The likes of "carpet"
and "floor tiles" were nonexistent in our vocabulary because they were unheard
of, just like how "iPods," "iPads," and "iPhones" were never in the English language until recent times. You don't miss what you don't know.

I still remember vividly that one of these mud houses collapsed in the middle of the night and killed one of my best friends.

There was no running water. There was no electricity. There was no gas.
A small river ran on the outskirts of the town. Legend had it that an American
half-caste priest, whom they called the Whiteman because of the color of his
skin, first discovered it. He was called Stewart. And the river was then named
after him.

Each household had a huge pot placed in the corner of the kitchen. This
was embedded in dried mud to keep the contents cool. This provided a cooled

water reservoir. Every morning, the children, as part of the household chores, would walk to River Stewart to fetch drinking water to fill the pot. The buckets filled with water were carried on the head, stabilized by a pad fashioned from a piece of cloth. Depending on the distance from your home to River Stewart, you could walk up to a mile or so with the bucket of water skillfully balanced on your head.

The moonlight and the stars were our streetlights. The spectacles of shooting stars were amazing. Kerosene lamps provided light at night in the homes. These generated a lot of heat and fumes. Imagine yourself trying to sleep in a small mosquito-infested confinement with one small window and a kerosene lamp to provide visibility. We did not know any better. And that is how it was.

Students and pupils studied at night on a small table and with the kerosene lamp as close to the books as possible. It is rather tough to think about it now, but it felt normal at the time and was not a big deal.

The climate was hot and tropical. Temperatures were up to 100°F (37.8°C), and with humidity, the conditions could become unbearable. There were two rainy seasons. The rest of the time it was dry. When it rained, it poured. Flooding was common because of the topography and the nature of the housing conglomerate. Not uncommonly, the kids would go out in the middle of the rainfall and waddle in the floodwater. It was fun. We had no idea that the floodwater carried excrement and dirt. Years later, in medical school, I studied how hookworm and cholera were passed on from one person to another by contact with infected matter. Such infected matter permeated the floodwater.

The harmattan weather was the coldest. Temperatures ranged from 60°–70°F (15°–21°C) during this time. This was a weather system wherein there was a reversal of wind blowing from North Africa southward over the Sahara Desert, carrying with it particles of sand from the desert. This weather was usually associated with Christmas. It would usually start in November and finish by March. These days, global warming has shifted the timing of this weather system.

During the harmattan, there was a feeling of joy since Christmas was just around the corner. This was the time when we would be treated with new clothes, shoes, and goodies. This was also the time when we were treated to expensive delicacies like chicken and goat meat. This was when you could also be spoiled with a whole chicken egg for yourself or have a Coca-Cola, Fanta, and other soft drinks. In contrast, on days that were outside the Christmas season, we ate mainly fish and game and drank water to quench our thirst.

Santa Claus was called Father Christmas and never appeared in person, or, I should say, he was never impersonated. You would see pictures of him on billboards in the big cities. Children never heard hype about Santa coming to their homes. We had no Christmas trees in our homes, but the radios played all kinds of Christmas songs. Despite all these apparent deficiencies, I still remember to this day how good Christmas was.

It is not uncommon for Ghanaians to speak at least one extra language. My small village was no exception. The language spoken there was Krobo. Travel fourteen miles west, and the language changed to Twi, and thirty miles south there was a completely different language, Eve. So most of my contemporaries were fluent in at least two languages. I speak five: English, French, and three Ghanaian languages.

Multilingualism is now known in medicine to delay the onset of Alzheimer's dementia. I cannot attest to this fact at that time in my village since there have been no retrospective controlled studies; however, I cannot recollect encountering glaring cases of early dementia. My father had vascular dementia in his nineties, and my mum had very mild age-related forgetfulness in her late eighties. They were both multilingual.

Most languages go into extinction as a result of emigration, migration, lack of a college curriculum for the language, and lack of development of new words to keep in touch with the modern world. Listen to young educated people in the street or on the radio, and one would immediately realize how the Krobo language is incapable of expressing common concepts. There are so many English words interjected into sentences that a whole conversation becomes half-English and half-Krobo. I personally find this very annoying because of the lack of purity in our language, which I believe sooner or later will be extinct.

Like most Western countries, the village mirrored religious tolerance that occurred in all parts of Ghana. Christians, Muslims, and pagans lived in harmony. Christmas and Ramadan were celebrated together. Religious holidays were mutually observed.

Christians made up about 60 percent, Muslims about 20 percent, and the remaining population was either pagan or had no religion.

The pagans worshipped small gods or deities. Even though this group made up a very small percentage of the population, it was the most feared. Their shrines were constructed with scary objects like parts of human skeletons, most commonly the skull, or skulls of large animals like lions or tigers. Each of these parts was meant to represent the special powers bestowed on that particular shrine. The shrine was further adorned with the blood of sacrificed animals like chickens and goats.

The caretakers of these shrines were the juju men. The juju man was usually scantily dressed either in a straw skirt or tattered clothes. He usually possessed a horse tail called an *ahuja*. The ahuja was the object used to transfer power from the deity to a person.

The visual representation of shrines was meant to instill fear in people and accord respect for the juju man.

The juju man was believed to treat all sorts of ailments. These included infertility, sickle cell disease, polio, abdominal pains, and fractures, to name a few. It seems to me that diseases that could not be explained by local knowledge were attributed to being caused by spirits. The juju man was able to intercede on behalf of the patient to fix the problem.

The juju man was accessible and inexpensive. He would collect some chickens and goats for his compensation. He also dwelled in the local community. The result of his healing did not matter. If he was successful, it was attributed to his powers. If he failed, it was the wish of the afflicting spirits to take a life.

One of my brothers was run over by a vehicle and fractured his tibia. My father took him to a juju man. The juju man's fee was one goat and one chicken. The chicken was used for the ritual. The juju man broke one of the chicken's legs and put it in a splint. Then he made small incisions on my brother's fracture site, rubbed in a concoction of a secret herbal preparation, and splinted his fractured leg. He asked that my brother stay at his compound for three months. After this period of time, he would untie the chicken's leg. If the chicken's fracture had healed, it meant my brother's fracture had also healed. And that was the case. My brother walked after three months. That was "wow" to the uninitiated and kudos to the juju man, but it is pure science learned through the generations and had nothing to do with having special healing powers.

That was the good side of the juju man. We quickly learned never to be on the wrong side of the shrine. They were revered because of the harm or death they could cause to others. If you were wronged by anyone for any reason and wanted to seek revenge, the shrine was your best bet. The juju man would give you all the options in his spiritual armory. These would range from making the person paralyzed to making him blind or die. The compensations to the shrine were usually live chickens or goats, some of which would be sacrificed for the ritual. Like many of my contemporaries, I never witnessed the end results of the juju men's wrath, but fear of what they could do to you always settled brawls if one party threatened the other about seeking a particular shrine to intercede.

If you were relatively rich, you could be accused of having your wealth through the help of the juju man. Desperate people approached them so they could become wealthy. This required rigorous rituals, some of which needed the provision of human body parts from anybody or from a close relative. The human heart, the head, or the genitals may be some of the offerings needed for the rituals. It was alleged that the patrons may be required to sleep in a casket for days or spend many nights in the cemetery. The end result was usually the provision of an animal by the juju man to the patron. Some of these animals were said to be huge pythons that the patron would take home and keep in a safe location. This animal was supposed to regurgitate endless amounts of money to the patron.

My father was a victim of such accusation. He was relatively wealthy from hard work. But somehow the gut feelings of the township were heard through the vines, saying that he may have acquired his wealth with the help of a shrine. He was not directly approached for confirmation, but indirectly the kids would spill the village's feelings on me and my siblings in the form of insults when they engaged us in a quarrel.

The Muslims were usually immigrants who came to settle in the village from northern Ghana or Nigeria for economic reasons. Their religion was accepted as any other kind, with no stigma. We enjoyed celebrating their Ramadan, which was usually associated with an abundance of food and exceptional generosity. By virtue of their Ramadan, they were considered the most magnanimous in the village.

The Muslim religion in the village also had special personalities who identified themselves as possessing special powers. We called them *malams*. The malams were powerful spiritual men who would provide you with special charms called talismans. They were basically pieces of dried goat or cow skin sewed into the shape of a heart with a piece of cowrie stuck in the center. A piece of the leather was fashioned into a string. This allowed you to wear it as a necklace.

The talisman was an object for protection against evil spirits. It was meant to annul any spiritual attacks from witchcraft or juju men. It provided safety and security to the wearer. Even though you could buy a talisman from any craft shop, the one provided by the malam was the only one that could give you that protection.

Like many of my friends, I wore a talisman for many years during my youth. My father detested it because it was not Christian. My belief was that I was protecting myself. It worked because I did not succumb to any attack from bad spirits, and the anxiety of not wearing it would have been worse than the presumed spiritual attack itself.

Village life was soaked in myths and beliefs that could get you sucked into taking actions that made onlookers and third parties think of you as being weird and ridiculous. I see this as human nature and not a village phenomenon.

The largest religious group in the village were the Christians. I would divide this into two main categories since they affected the lives of the villagers in different manners. There were three orthodox churches: Roman Catholic, Presbyterian, and Apostolic. Then there were myriad spiritual churches run by so-called men or women of God.

The spiritual churches flourished on the myths and beliefs of villagers. They were usually located in private huts and compounds of the owners. Their membership could range anywhere from ten to a couple of hundred. The membership size was in direct proportion to the number of purported miracles in the form of healings under the owners' belts. The services were associated with characteristic drumming, singing, and dancing and would go on for hours. It was not uncommon to hear them go on all night.

They provided a lively church service and then a session of private consultations and healing. The private consultations and healing sessions were very popular. Typically the spiritual person would pray with you for a few minutes. After that, you would be told of a vision they had seen of you. These could range from how you would become rich and famous in the future to your impending doom. They could tell you who your enemies in your family were. Sicknesses that you were afflicted with could be attributed to a witch in the family. In fact, they had explanations for every misfortune in your life.

I remember that one of my brothers was afflicted with polio. He was three years old. He went to bed the previous night in good health. The following morning, he woke up paralyzed in one leg. One would think the first place to call would have been the hospital, but the elders from the village gathered to provide the best solution for a cure. One of them recalled a good spiritual person who was said to have made someone walk after paralysis. After we had located her in a remote village, my brother was transported there. The villages were linked by footpaths only, and his transportation was shared among the elders, who took turns carrying him on their backs to the spiritualist.

The spiritualist told my family not to worry. The paralysis was because of bad spirits. He would walk again within six months with prayers and fasting. My brother had to stay with the spiritualist for that period of time. My mother stayed with him.

For the special prayer sessions, my parents had to provide candles and an imported anointment oil pseudo-named Florida water. They fasted, prayed, and hoped for many months. Six months passed, and he was still paralyzed.

Finally, they gave up, following the advice of our Catholic priest, who suggested my brother be taken to the Catholic hospital nearby. He was transported to the Catholic hospital in the regional capital. Soon after he was admitted, he underwent some form of surgical procedure and was fitted with calipers and rehabilitated. One day we visited him in the hospital. I saw him in his calipers and crutches walking for the first time in about twelve months. It was a tearful moment to see the pride on his face at being able to walk again.

My personal experience with spiritualists was not without drama. I may have been seven or eight years old. One day my mother came home after a consultation with a renowned spiritualist. She was vividly distressed. Then I remember a closed-door meeting with my father. Their body language made it obvious that her distress had something to do with me.

Shortly after, my father held his usual family meeting at dawn. These dawn meetings occurred when the kids did something wrong and needed to be reprimanded. Everyone would be woken from their sleep and assembled in my father's room. Then my father would lead the prayer in the Catholic fashion, using the rosary and reciting "Hail Mary, full of grace..." several times. Then he would systematically spell out all the things we had done wrong. He would put in place corrective measures, which could include caning, pinching of the ear until you cried, or omitting one meal. The meetings were dreaded. In order for these meetings not to happen often we'd put on our best behavior.

The family meeting held this time was different. My name was mentioned in the prayers, and the attention focused on me soon after. It became apparent that my mother had received bad news about me when she went to see the spiritualist. She was told that the witches in the village were going to sacrifice me for their Christmas. I was going to die on Christmas Day, which was about three months away. She was asked to take me to the church for a ritual that would annul the power of the witches and prevent my demise.

The news sent all gathered in the dawn meeting into severe anxiety and distress. My siblings sobbed and panicked. The days following this were somber for everyone.

Within a few days, I was taken to the compound of the spiritualist, which was located in the next village, about five miles away. It was a big compound with a gravel ground and pockets of unkempt grass scattered all over. In the center was a tree stump, on top of which was mounted a big cross, made from the odum tree, adorned with a piece of dirty white cloth. Surrounding the compound were a few rooms made of mud and thatched roofing. The flooring was mud, and there were tiny windows covered with slabs of wood. The toilet was not too far out in the bush. It was a big hole in the ground covered with wood planks to allow for squatting and relieving oneself. The pit and its environs were full of flies, and once in a while, depending on the direction of the wind, its stench would blow to bless the entire compound.

My mother and I were given one of these rooms to stay in for the ritual, which had been planned to last for one week. We had a meeting with the spiritualist in her room. She was an elderly woman with gray hair neatly braided and tied down. Her head was partly wrapped in a multicolored silk scarf. She wore a white gown that almost touched the ground. She was calm in her composure in a fashion that convinced me she was a woman of God. She spoke softly. She had other women seated with her, also dressed in long gowns, and their heads were covered with a piece of white calico. These were her aides, called the church mothers.

My mother introduced me as the son proclaimed to be sacrificed. Then she opened her bag and presented to the spiritualist all the items she had requested to perform the ritual. These were a piece of white calico, a brand-new shaving blade, a roll of black hair-braiding thread, Florida water, a bunch of candles, and a sum of money. The items were examined and approved with a head nod. The ritual was detailed to my mother, and the session ended with a long, loud prayer in a language I had never heard before. Later on, my mother told me they had been speaking in tongues.

The following six days, they woke us up at the third cockcrow, which was supposed to be about 5:00 a.m. They would form a human circle around me. I would be on my knees. Then they prayed, usually in tongues, for me until sunrise, which was about 6:00 a.m.

My mother and I underwent seven days of fasting from sunrise until sunset. We were allowed only water during the fast and one big meal at the end of each day. The long days in this compound were spent doing absolutely nothing. I filled them with thoughts of my demise and how I was going to miss my family if the spiritualist intervention failed. Prayers were scheduled at midday and soon after the fast.

On the seventh day, after the dawn prayer, I was escorted to the outside toilet with a bowl of cold water. While I was standing on the toilet, one of the church mothers scrubbed my whole naked body with a sponge made from a beaten string plant soaked in cold water. The water dripped into the toilet below me, making a sound like rainwater pouring onto very wet mud. This sound and the stench swelling out below me created the most disgusting experience I had ever had. But this initial process was meant to cleanse me of all the evil spirits.

After the bath, I was dried with a clean towel and wrapped from head to toe in the white calico my mother had brought. A slit was made in the calico at my eye level to allow me to see. The black thread was wrapped over the calico to secure it in place. Then I was escorted to one corner of the compound. It was, by this time, full of people who came to witness my deliverance. While standing, they prayed and prayed. It was very loud. Some of them prayed in tongues. It went on for a long time.

At the end of the prayer, the spiritualist was handed the new shaving blade. While praying and commanding and calling the name of Jesus in the rhetorical fashion, she cut through the black thread in several areas, releasing me from the bondage of the witchcraft. It was an emotional moment for my mother, whom I heard burst into uncontrollable crying. I knew at the time that I was finally saved from the bondage of the devil.

Then the white calico was unwrapped from me, releasing my naked body. It was at an age when I was aware of my private parts, so I felt very embarrassed at that point. I was instructed to run to the center of the court and embrace the cross.

It was a very cold harmattan morning. All I could hear was the uninterrupted chirping of the birds in the surrounding forest. I was very cold, and together with the extreme anxiety I was going through, I felt the goose pimples sticking out of my skin like a porcupine. As I ran across the compound to my salvation at the cross of Jesus, the whole compound roared in prayers from all who had gathered to witness my salvation.

Whether I believed the presumption or not, I was liberated, and that was all that mattered. At least it cured my anxiety about dying. It relieved the stress of my parents about losing a son at a tender age. My siblings smiled with contentment when I returned home. Christmas passed, and I did not die; it was the best one I had ever had. I was treated to a lot of goat meat as it was usually tradition to slaughter a goat for Christmas.

The Apostolic Church, Presbyterian Church, and Roman Catholic Church were the churches with very little drama. My father was a staunch Roman Catholic. We were all baptized in the Catholic faith.

We went to church every Sunday. It was a must. If any child skipped the Sunday service, he or she was denied dinner as a form of punishment. But it was fun going to church. It was the only time we adorned ourselves with our new clothes and wore shoes. It was a show-off day. We would never miss out on Sunday Mass.

The Catholic priests at the time were European or American whites. The priest recited the service partly in Latin and partly in English, which none of us understood. But the sermon was translated into our local dialect.

Our English names were called Christian names. A few months after giving birth, parents would register their children for baptism. During the ceremony, the priest would assign the child a name from the Bible. It would be a random name selected by the priest alone. Nobody knew what name you would be assigned until the ceremony was over. The priest would say, for instance, "John, I baptize you in the name of Jesus." A scribe would be close by to record the given Christian name. A baptismal card would be issued to the parents at the end of the ceremony. In it would be written the Christian name, the traditional name, and the last name, in that order. There would also be a section for birth dates. Since there were no birth certificates issued at the time of birth, the dates were usually inaccurate. And this was how we all got our English names.

The village had two schools. One was Roman Catholic and the other Presbyterian. Patronage was dependent on one's religious orientation. Each of them had a primary school from class one to class six and a middle school, form one to form four.

Primary education started at age six. There was no preschool. Since birth dates were inaccurate, there was no way to know when the child was ready to start class one. However, the teachers cleverly designed an anatomical means of determining maturity to commence class one.

When the parents determined that the child was ready to start class one, the child would be presented to the school headmaster. He would eyeball the child, and if he was not sure, he would ask the child to pass one arm over the head and touch the opposite ear. If the child was able to touch the opposite ear with the hand, it was a de facto qualification to commence class one. This test became so popular that children like me, eager to start school, were constantly checking their readiness themselves. One can imagine how this created a lot of late starters or never starters in those who were anatomically challenged, like short people or those with achondroplasia.

The village educational system had a ten-year duration. Most of my contemporaries, including some of my brothers and sisters, did not have any further education after the age of sixteen. You would be awarded a certificate of completion of form four, and it was considered a great achievement. Further education was called secondary education, which had a path to university or technical training.

To have further education meant a boarding school in bigger towns and a lot of money from parents. Only rich folks could afford to send their children to secondary school. Even then it was limited to children with high academic achievements and good behavior and had to be recommended by the teachers. This was how I came into the limelight for my dad and was given the opportunity to have further education.

Today, when I visit the village that I call my hometown, it does not feel the same. I feel like a total stranger. It has tripled its original size and is filled with total strangers. Or perhaps I am their stranger! Most of my friends and contemporaries have passed on. Occasionally grandchildren and great-grandchildren of my contemporaries will approach me and introduce themselves. I sometimes hardly recognize them.

My old primary school has recently been a national news item as it has deteriorated to the point that the school children and teachers are competing with snakes and bats for space.

But the silver lining of progress is that the village now has electricity and decent pipe-borne water. To me this is huge progress. It would have made life much easier had these amenities been present during my time.

Chapter 2

PARENTS

MOM

My mother called herself an orphan anytime she experienced a nostalgic feeling about her late mother, who had passed away when she was still a baby. Her father, who was a wealthy goldsmith in a neighboring village called Asesewa, had raised her. Like other wealthy men of that era, he had other children, my mother's half sisters and half brothers, whom until recent times I had known as and called uncles and aunts.

From memory of photos my mother kept in her safe box, which she would proudly open only on occasions of festivity, I was able to figure out that she married my father at a very tender age, probably in her late teens and probably through an arranged marriage. Her loving, rich father, who wanted to make sure his half-orphaned daughter found a comfortable matrimonial home, sought a promising young man in the surrounding village and found my young enterprising father, who was a customer of his jewelry business. It was a perfect fit, and my mother became my father's third wife.

Like most girls in the village, my mother did not receive any formal education. She was proud to count to ten in English. However, her intellectual prowess made her a very successful businesswoman, surpassing all of her contemporaries in the village.

She chose baking as her profession, one that seemed to have been passed on in her family through generations like a dominant gene. She excelled. She had a string of wholesalers throughout the surrounding villages. I remember a huge clay oven in our home, loaded with dry wood and lit every morning. I still have the sensation of the smell of fermenting bread molded in greased aluminum cans scattered throughout our home. It was the only bread factory in the area, and it was successful because my mother had a supposed secret formula that made her bread taste extra special.

Mom was from the Ga tribe in the Greater Accra Region but was born and raised in Krobo tribe environs. Hence the Krobo language was her first language, which she spoke to her children. She was also compelled to speak Ga and Twi, broadening the horizons of her baking business.

Mom had a cool and calm demeanor, a trait I inherited. She was never angry and never angered anyone. A woman of few words, she spoke softly and firmly and never beat around the bush. She was kind and generous. Her kind heart won her love and admiration from both her children and her neighbors. She was affectionately called Maa Karley, a nickname unique to her that she rightly earned through her generosity and used to grow and promote her baking business. Her brand was Maa Karley Bread, and it was preferred over any other bread in the locality.

Maa Karley was blessed with children in abundance. Not only did she have two sets of twins, but she in fact had twelve children in total. She could have continued had it not been for the last delivery being deemed difficult and ending up as a cesarean with a tubal ligation.

Her first birth was a set of fraternal twins, Agatha and Agnes. A stillbirth, a girl, followed them. Then came elder brother Tawiah. He was born disabled and mentally challenged. He was mute and had night blindness. He did not have any meaningful kind of life. He died from tuberculosis in his thirties. Then two sisters followed in quick succession, Korko and Mamle. I came in sixth position. Three brothers—Tetteh, Teye, and Narh—followed me. The last born was a fraternal set of twins who came by a cesarean section, Attah and Larweh. The boy, Larweh, was predicted not to survive, and he died within a few weeks.

Attah, the girl, survived. Her no-nonsense character makes one think she has the life of two people.

There was, and still is, a high infant mortality rate and a high maternal mortality rate in Africa mostly because of inaccessibility to modern medicine. Traditional birth attendants who acquired their skills through coaching by their parents tended to most of Mom's deliveries at home. They did not have any formal medical training. These days, traditional birth attendants have progressively been recognized by modern medicine as important players in maternal care and childcare in a society where there are too few trained medical personnel. They are now being trained with basic skills to recognize and refer early potential medical problems. A home delivery in my mom's era was scary business.

Growing up in a large family with a wide sibling age gap was quite an amazing experience. Since I was the sixth child, my childhood interactions with my siblings were limited to only those within my immediate age group. I never had any playtime experience with my eldest sisters, who had already matured and left home. They visited on festive occasions and brought us goodies. Today, as our parents are deceased, they naturally assumed the role of parents, and the younger siblings accorded them that respect.

Of all my mom's children, I felt I caused the most fuss. I did not toe the line. I refused to comply with the norm. I did not like to help in my father's mechanic shop because I did not want my hands dirty with engine oil. I requested to drink porridge for breakfast every morning instead of the usual breakfast of fish and a corn-based meal called *kenkey*. I refused to eat from the same bowl as my brother as was the norm. When I was forced to do it, I ate so fast that my younger brother would give up and start crying. I would hear my mother scolding him for being a slow eater. I self-inflicted an allergy to the common evening meal, a cassava meal called *fufu*. My mother went out of her way to prepare a special replacement dish just for me. Sometimes I would frustrate my mother when I thought there were too many of us for the few things that were at our disposal, like food, presents, and so on. I would tell her we were too many. Her answer was always the same: "Had it not been that way, you would not have been born." That always shut me up.

She wanted me to be a policeman. I said no. I wanted to be a doctor.

With all my fuss, I felt that I was destined to be the leader of the family in the future or, better still, the one who would lift the family out of poverty. You can call it similar to the biblical Moses, and my mother would have said you were right. This intuition, I suppose, was purely because of my academic excellence and good school reports from my teachers. I was the best student right from class one.

My mother keenly followed my progress at school. One day she visited me in the boarding school, which was located in the regional capital, Koforidua, and brought with her food and presents. At home I was called Kweku John, but in the boarding school, my friends just called me John Awah. When she arrived at the school, she asked to see her son, Kweku John. She was heartbroken and dismayed when none of the students knew anyone by that name. She spent the whole day in the school looking for me. She finally gave up and gave the food and present she had brought for me to one of the students. Just as she was exiting from the school gate, one of the students who knew her through the bread business approached her. She told him she could not find me. Within minutes, my friend located me. She was in tears when I arrived.

Mom enjoyed relatively good health throughout her life. I was able to provide my Mom with the necessary support that enabled her to enjoy a very good quality of life that improved her longevity to a great extent. She exceeded the statistical life expectancy in the village of fifty-five years for men and sixty-five years for women by far. I played a very significant role in resolving the unexpected health hazards that afflicted her during her life span. Her family had the longevity gene, and with me removing the health encumbrances that befell her, she was able to realize her full life span or close to it.

She was about sixty-six inches tall and carried an average weight of about two hundred pounds. She was physically active by virtue of village life, where walking was the most common means of transport.

In her late fifties, her vision began to deteriorate. This started with floaters in her visual fields, and within a few years, she could hardly see. One day I heard on the radio about a mercy ship that docked in Cape Coast, a town about two hundred miles from the village. At the time, I was in my late teens and was an avid reader. I went through the newspapers to discover that the mercy ship had doctors from the United States. They were treating people with blindness. There were many testimonies from patients with restored vision. I was delighted to break the news to my mom and dad.

My dad gave the go-ahead that Mom should go for this miraculous cure. With the little money available, no hotel arrangement made, and accompanied by one of my sisters, we arrived in Cape Coast after a whole day. There we spent the night in an open camp on the beach. The following morning, the white men, as we called them, came on land to triage the patients. Then Mom was transported in a small boat onto the ship for treatment. The wait seemed very long to me. They brought her back after a few hours with a huge patch on one eye. She was told to stay in the camp for the patch to be removed the following day.

"Will Mom also get this miracle cure?" I muttered to myself. She went back into the ship the following day, and this time she was returned to shore without the white bandage across the face but with a big smile. Her vision was restored. Though the un-operated eye still had fuzzy vision, she was happy to be able to see again with one eye.

Later on in my career, I gathered that the surgery she had had was cataract surgery. In retrospect, I can now see how cataracts blinded many unfortunate souls in the village and put their remaining years in darkness.

When Mom was in her seventies, she had another health challenge. This time it was a back pain that progressively got worse. I was in my late twenties, pursuing postgraduate training in medicine in England. I went home for Christmas vacation. It was a very sad Christmas. Mom was paralyzed in both legs and could no longer walk because of the back problem.

I took her to the only neurosurgeon in the country, who recommended surgery. This neurosurgeon had a reputation for bad outcomes. I was very hesitant. I asked myself how he could operate on Mom without telling me what the diagnosis was. There was no MRI scan in the country, and his diagnosis was based on a simple, plain X-ray of her back. I decided against the surgery because of the risk of her becoming completely paralyzed or dying from the surgery.

When vacation time was over and I was leaving, Mom cried so much that it put chills in my spine. She asked if I was leaving her in that state and if I might come to meet her again. My return trip to England was packed with sadness. I cried. I asked myself what I could do to help her.

Upon my return, I asked my boss if he could help me bring my mom to England to be treated in the hospital where I worked. He was pleased to help. Then a very long visa process to get Mom to England ensued. She was denied the visa initially on grounds of bringing a potentially dangerous disease to England as well as coming to take advantage of the free health care of the country. Then I went through the appeal process with letters from experts in communicable diseases in England and proof of funding to pay for her health care.

Visas were eventually granted to both her and my sister, who would accompany her to serve as a chaperone. At this time, she was wheelchair bound. Special arrangements were made with the airline. She arrived eventually at my home in England. It was a relief, but it was also the first step of her uncertain outcome.

The following days were full of medical consultations, imaging, and tissue biopsy. Within a short time, it was concluded that she had developed spinal tuberculosis. Then she was referred to another doctor specializing in infectious diseases. She was given multiple pills to combat the infection, a regime that lasted for six months.

Within four to six weeks, her back pain had significantly subsided, and she gradually regained strength in her legs. To her amazement, she was able to stand for the first time in many months. She took her first steps like a baby who has started to learn how to walk. She graduated from wheelchair to walking and never looked back. Her other blind eye was operated on to remove a dense cataract. She became a new woman.

She returned to Ghana after eight months. The arrival hall was full of family members to receive her. They all burst into a mixture of cheers and cries when they saw her walking for the first time.

Mom developed diabetes in her seventies, a condition that ran in her family. At this time, I was a full-fledged physician. Even though I was not living in Ghana, I monitored her remotely. I assigned her a physician, a close friend of the family. She received good medical care.

Mom enjoyed her last years in a home I built for her in Accra. She was fully served and supported by her children and grandchildren until her natural demise from complications of diabetes. She died at almost ninety. I was content that, unlike her contemporaries in the village, her life had been lived in full.

DAD

Dad was born into a royal family of a tribe in the Greater Accra Region in Ghana, the Shai tribe. His great-grandfather was alleged to have resisted and fought the British during their early incursions in Ghana in the slave trade business. Having quickly gained a nickname by the locals, Ahwa, meaning "the Warrior," he became the leader in the fight against the colonial invaders. This earned him the position of the first ruler and king of the Shai tribe. The chieftaincy has since been passed on to the descendants of Nene Awah I. The name Ahwa went through many metamorphoses because of the difficulty of its pronunciation and eventually became Anglicized into Awah. To this day, this name is unique to my family in Ghana.

The chieftaincy alternated among the siblings of Nene Awah I. My dad's children were next in line for the throne when I was an adolescent, and his task was to produce and nurture an eligible male child for the job.

Dad was slender and tall. Towering about six feet two inches tall and weighing about 180 pounds, he was a physically prominent figure. He had a biweekly appointment to keep his hair neat and a wrinkleless face that made his age difficult to guess. His signature outfit was British-fashioned khaki shorts and a jumper. He was known for his strict and organized character. He spoke with the utmost authority. He was very well respected.

He did not have any formal education, but his exposure to white folks during his apprenticeship allowed him to gather a few English words and phrases. He exhibited these expressions in his day-to-day work in such a way that unsuspecting clients thought he was fluent in English. Many of his contemporaries, who were also illiterates, thought he was so fluent in English that they yearned for the day when they could hear him interact with a fluent English interlocutor.

He did his apprenticeship in motor mechanics in a workshop owned by a British company in Accra. After graduating, he moved out of the big city to the country to set up a workshop. He found the village Oterkpolu in the eastern region of Ghana, a small village located at a T-junction linking two major towns to another major market town. This strategic location ensured a frequent flow of vehicular traffic that fed his workshop. His became the only mechanic shop covering a very wide area. He became known as Papa Fitter. This became his trade name.

He was successful in passing on this trade to most of his offspring. It was not for me. I did not want my fingers dirty, and I refused to learn it.

Dad became very successful by virtue of his work. By all accounts, he was the wealthiest man in the locality. Not only was he the only one who owned a private car, but he also owned multiple commercial vehicles. He dominated the transport business with his vehicles. Additionally, he set up corn mills in multiple villages and monopolized that business for many years.

His house was the grandest. It consisted of eight rooms made of mud and arranged in a rectangular fashion around a huge compound, a car garage, and two stand-alone kitchens.

As befitting a wealthy man, all the rooms had cement floors and were roofed with aluminum sheets. Each of these rooms was meant for a wife and her children. The kitchens were also made of mud, roofed with aluminum, and had cement flooring.

His own private living quarters were a suite. This was two rooms joined together, one being a sitting area and the other an adjoining bedroom. It was popularly called a chamber and hall. It was a dwelling with connotations of wealth.

The quarters were fully furnished with expensive, comfortable furniture meant for important visitors. On one wall was a huge pendulum clock whose hourly chimes could be heard from all four corners of the compound. Then there was a kerosene refrigerator, the only one in the village, to provide chilled water and soft drinks for his guests. To complete the décor was a huge beautiful wooden chest that stored glassware and cutlery. On top of the chest was a big two-speaker transistor radio with white lace material placed on it to simulate a bourgeoisie-like appearance. To keep the living area clean and tidy, he made a special roster for the kids so there was no confusion whose turn it was to clean.

Many businesses in Africa mirror the life span of the owner. This could probably be because of lack of education coupled with lack of planning for the future. This was what happened to my dad. My mother was my dad's third of his five wives. This meant I was born when his business had passed its peak of success. My generation of his kids witnessed the decline of his wealth to the extent that I was among the last two of his children whom he could afford to sponsor for a secondary education. This was the time when, on reflection, dad was getting older and declining in steam. With proper planning, he should have been retiring from active labor or even having more children. The remaining children felt shortchanged and still do today. Their lives would have been much easier had they been exposed to further education.

He was a strict disciplinarian who held a monthly disciplinary meeting. The children named it "court." This was usually held at dawn in his living quarters. In attendance would be all the kids and wives. With his rosary in hand, Dad would typically begin the court session with prayers in the Roman Catholic fashion. We would recite many prayers of "Hail Mary, full of grace…" Then he would reiterate a sermon from a recent Sunday church service and ask for a short prayer from one of his wives, followed by the usual amen that would conclude the prayer session.

Following this would be a recounting from him of all the wrongs that had happened since the last meeting. Then he would assign the appropriate admonishment and punishment for the wrongdoers. It was a form of micro theocracy. You accepted your fault. You did what you were told. And you did not talk back.

A raffia cane was always strategically placed in this room to serve as a deterrent for mischievous behavior, though lashes were very common. Even if the kid came home to report of being lashed in school by the teacher for doing the wrong thing, that kid would receive another lash from Dad for being mischievous in school in the first place.

Dad was very religious, a staunch Roman Catholic. He never missed Sunday Mass, so that was his expectation for all his kids. At a typical Sunday Mass, he would be among the first to arrive in church and sit in the back pews. Then one by one, he would watch the arrivals of his kids and make a mental notation of who did not show up. Missing Sunday Mass was punishable by caning or forfeiting a meal.

My father was very generous. He gave a lot of money and gifts to the church and the catholic school. He was appointed the president of many associations in the church and the school and was the obvious choice to chair many of their functions.

Dad had five wives and over thirty children. We all lived together in the same compound house. Each wife and her children were assigned a room. So in each room was an elevated bed with a homemade, hard cotton mattress. The mother shared the bed with the youngest kids. The rest of the kids slept on a straw mat laid on the floor. Pillows were a luxury. So kids slept on a bare straw mat using their fisted hands as pillows.

I gathered that the reason for polygamy was wealth, more wealth, and prestige. The man's role was to provide food and shelter for the family—probably an animal instinct, I suppose. The society looked down on anyone who could not fulfill this responsibility. So if you had the money, you could perform this function without fail. It was also evident in the village that the poorer you were, the fewer number of wives you could afford to marry.

Then with more wives came many kids. Since farming labor was all manual, the more kids one had, the more hands were on deck. The larger families were able to turn out more farm yield, which meant more money for the household.

Then with all the wives and kids looking well, respect and reverence were accorded to the head of the household. This may sound simplistic, but that was how I saw it.

Dad had impeccable health. He resisted aging. He drove his car until he was in his nineties. Even in his later years, when his kids nicknamed him Old Man, he would frown on it. He aged gracefully.

He had a personal physician whom he visited regularly in the regional capital. He was hospitalized one time for acute urine retention, which resulted in prostate surgery. His life ended with severe pain and suffering, which gives me nightmares to this day.

I was a fourth-year medical student, a half-baked doctor, when this happened. Money was tight because of fierce competition against his business. I was called from school and told that he was ill. When I went to see him, he was in severe respiratory distress and was very swollen in his face and feet. He was clearly suffering. As a medical student, I quickly knew he had a heart problem. There was absolutely no money to take him to the hospital. The thought of it today makes me realize how poor we were at the time.

With the little money I had on me, I went to the nearest pharmacy, which was located in the regional capital, fourteen miles away. I bought a handful of water pills and digoxin, which I learned in medical school was used to treat heart failure. I gave instructions to Mom on how to administer the medications, and I left for school. It was the best and only thing I could do at that moment. Today, when I think about it, I say to myself, "Wow. Was that the only treatment available for acute heart failure? What about intensive care management with its bells and whistles, which I currently practice, to find the cause of heart failure and administer the right treatment?"

Life was cheap at the time. One was lucky to live without being ill. Have a catastrophic illness, and you would have no chance of survival. Usually this would be attributed to the work of a bad spirit as retribution.

Dad died after one week. Many people who found themselves in a similar situation as Dad had no chance of survival.

As businesses mirrored the life span of the owner, we were poor at the time of his demise. There was no money to bury him. It became my responsibility to find the money. Being a fourth-year medical student, I was fortunate to be a friend with one doctor called Big J. He happened to be the wealthiest among all the junior doctors. I approached him to lend me the burial money. He sympathetically gave me the money after listening to my story. When I tried to pay him back after the funeral, he refused to take the money he had lent me.

Unlike Mom, Dad did not benefit from my medical expertise. I could have done a lot more for him if his sickness had come after my Hippocratic oath. Maybe I could have added a few more years to his life if I had been in a better financial situation. Every day I live with the thought that even though he died in his nineties, he did not benefit from life extension afforded by modern medicine. His longevity gene took him there. But he was still shortchanged. He could have lived a bit longer.

Chapter 3

EXTENDED FAMILY STRUCTURE AND SIBLINGS

One could always wonder why, with all the wealth, wives, and children he had enjoyed, Dad's life ended in a bit of a financial pickle. A postmortem of the family dynamics would explain this tragedy. The revelations of such an analysis would guard his progeny from repeating the same mistakes and mitigate its shortcomings.

Most Africans have a network of uncles, aunts, grandmothers, grandfathers, cousins, and so on. This does not stop there. Each of the aforementioned also has extended links of his or her own. All these people belong to one family. The purist in the family would attempt to detail the exact nature of the connection between one family member and the other. This could sometimes send one's brain twisting to follow the link. The links could be so complicated that it is sometimes sufficient to introduce a family member as an uncle, aunt, or cousin without further explanation.

The family has the inherent duty to help each member. This creates a buffer zone for the family unit, notwithstanding the accompanying good sides and many bad sides. When it works out well, the less fortunate ones have the ability to ease off the intensity of their problems with the help of the relatively well-off ones. The relatively well-offs are constantly bombarded with demands from the less fortunate. Because this is the expectation, there is no shame about it, and it works fine.

For example, it is not unusual to send your two-year-old child to another part of the country to be brought up by another family member who was not fortunate to have been blessed with a child. This eases off the financial burden of the biological parents and provides comfort for the child and the adopting family.

I was a great beneficiary of this system of extended family when I was less fortunate in my early years. Today, I feel obliged and blood-bound to give back to the system that delivered me into the world of haves, and I feel very proud to perform my duty sincerely.

After the extended family came my core family. In my case, it was composed of Dad, his five wives, and his children. Because of rampant infant mortality and early childhood mortality in the family, it is difficult for me to know exactly how many children Dad had. However, the estimation of the living at some point was in the range of thirty or more, which by all counts is excessive but commensurate to his peak wealth.

So I have many half brothers and half sisters. All lived in the same compound at some point, in generation groups. I was a product of a third wife and was the sixth born of my mother, so I belonged to the generation in the descending loop of Dad's peak wealth.

Usually one would expect brothers and sisters to share same childhood experiences when they lived together. In this case, it felt strange when your elder brother or sister was much more matured and had already left home before you were born. The generation gap created did not allow for the same brotherly or sisterly connection one would expect between siblings. Today, that phenomenon has created a scene making the earlier generation appear to be the parents of the younger generation.

Within the generation, though, every sibling from the different mothers got along well with one another. It was very harmonious. The wives lived together in the same compound, but each one slept in her assigned room with her kids. They took weekly turns to share Dad's living quarters. There was no animosity among them. Or if there ever had been any rifts among them, they were kept under a tight lid, and none of the children knew.

The wife sharing Dad's quarters for the week would be the one responsible to cook for Dad. There was a set time when his food should be ready. He was the only one who ate on a table; everyone else would have their food set on the mud floor.

His dining table was a piece of locally made rectangular furniture made from the *wawa* tree, measuring about two feet by eighteen inches and eighteen inches tall. It had to be set in a particular fashion: soup or stew placed on the right, the carbohydrate dish placed on the left, and water placed away from the sitting position, in a triangular fashion. Any deviation from this pattern, and you would be asked to correct it, or it would be noted for the next court session.

The formal education given to the kids in the family was very limited. There was a premise and undertone that the women did not need any rigorous education. The fact that they were going to be married and looked after by their husbands justified this assertion. Hence, analyzing the family, women's education was scant, and most of them did not have further education beyond the age of sixteen after graduating from basic education. Those who were well motivated to get further education attended vocational schools to study secretarial or catering courses.

The men had their professions already carved out for them. After their basic education at sixteen, they took after Dad's profession and became good mechanics. A handful had further vocational education to become teachers.

In retrospect, the professional aspiration of the family was set at a very low standard, but it was the best at the time and on par with or superior to most of our contemporaries.

I have witnessed the deaths of some of my brothers and sisters. There were a lot of early deaths. They were very painful because I did not understand what was going on. Usually they were attributed to a bad spirit or witchcraft. From my recollection, aided by my personal analysis by virtue of my profession as a doctor, they died from sickle cell disease, alcoholism, cancer, tuberculosis, and convulsions.

Some of the elder siblings never showed up again after leaving home. They simply disappeared.

One particular half brother who was my favorite was called Teye. He was in his twenties when I was about six or seven years old. When I knew him, he already had a below-the-knee amputation. He mobilized with a pair of crutches. He was undeterred by this disability. I remember him challenging his friends in a racing competition, crutches against legs. He was well opinionated. He was held in high esteem as the best auto mechanic in the village. He was a rebel and always opposing Dad's authority. He also spoke French in addition to English. I felt it was cool to learn French, and that was how I took to the French language.

After his basic education at sixteen, he attended a technical school to study engineering. With his engineering background, he performed many cool things in the house. He manufactured a homemade doorbell. It was the first and only in the village, which he fixed in Dad's living quarters. He introduced me to the telephone. He connected a wire from his room to his friend's room in the adjacent compound and was able to communicate with a telephone receiver. To me, he was the frontier to the future.

With one leg and his crutches, he drove Dad's stick-shift car one day when Dad was in church. It was very complicated to maneuver the clutch, accelerator, brakes, and gear with one leg and a crutch. This was what he did. With me in the passenger seat at the time, we ended up in a ditch not too far from the house. Missing Sunday Mass and ditching Dad's only car was a real double jeopardy!

The coolest above all was his talent as an illusionist. He performed many magical shows in the village. This was the thing I really wanted to learn. He always told me I needed to learn it from the dwarfs. These were mythical small people who, we believed, lived in the forest and possessed lots of spiritual powers.

He was a very popular personality in the village. Tragically, he died prematurely, in his thirties, from what I think was a complication of cancer of the muscle and bone called osteosarcoma. That was the reason for his leg amputation to begin with.

Other than the core family in this polygamy system, there was the micro core family, which was comprised of all the siblings belonging to one mother. The saying that "blood is thicker than water" perfectly describes the cohesion in this unit. Even though we felt we belonged to one family, there appeared to be stronger bonds among the siblings of the same mother. That makes sense and is rooted in biology. This cohesion is manifested in expressions of loyalty and sharing. As adults, it has resulted in who gets what first when I have something to share or whom I should go to first when I have a problem.

Black sheep can tear families apart if not managed well. Like most families, we had a few and fell victim to the black sheep drama. The ripple effects of this black sheep phenomenon still manifest today.

We had one male and one female black sheep. The male, the eldest in the family, was married with kids and still housed himself and his family in one room in the family compound. I did not understand why he did not move out with his family. For reasons unknown to me, he became very cantankerous toward Dad. The animosity created a huge rift between his family and other dwellers. Everyone ganged up against them. He became uncomfortable and fled. He was considered an outcast during the planning of Dad's final days and was excluded from all family activities.

The female had her grudge toward Mom. She belonged to new age religious groups that prophesied and gave explanations for every misfortune that afflicted their followers. In this case, she was unable to bear children. Her religious group explained to her that her womb was tied down by the power of the witchcraft practiced by her mom. Her mom was my mom too. She began to adulterate the minds of some of my siblings. Some believed her. Being a medical student at the time, I stepped in to protect Mom. I said to the woman that the reason was full of crap and had no scientific basis. So we became instant enemies. Most of my siblings believed me, and a few believed her. Then ensued many years of fighting among the believers of the opposite camps. Today, reality has dawned. In vitro fertilization, not invented at the time, would have solved this problem. Mom would not have been accused of witchcraft.

So my family is huge, spanning multiple generations and obeying the prevalent statistics of short life expectancies, being fifty-five to sixty-five years, each member with a trade, the bar of professional expectations being set so low and usually met, and happily living in our small unchallenged world. Weak covalent bonds among us and a lack of leadership from the older generation led to poor financial and estate planning to consolidate Dad's multiple properties and businesses. We were rich but poor. We were found wanting when the time came to take responsibility for Dad's calling. Too many people in one pot do not usually translate into wealth and can actually be disastrous.

It makes good sense that I was born into this family. I have probably made some contributions that may have averted disastrous consequences.

Chapter 4

CHILDHOOD

Anytime the question is posed about the earliest childhood year one can remember, the results are varied and interesting. It ranges from three years to seven years. For me, I can remember vividly the period of self-identification. I remember when I roamed around the home with no clothes on. I remember when we used to wash our bodies in the open with no shame. I remember when I began to feel shy about exposing my bare body to the general public. I remember my first day in school. So I can recall my childhood from around the age of about four years.

Children have no say in where they are born or whom they are born to. Some children are born to parents who do not deserve to have children, and others are born in refugee camps. Some are born in the remotest villages and others in the slums of rich countries. A few fortunate ones are born to the well-offs or even into monarchies. And some potentially well-deserving parents are unable to have children.

To be fair, children are not given a fair chance from the starting line. They accept the premise and make the best of it. What really matters is what one does with the situation in which one finds him- or herself. Look around the world, and you will notice that great people did not necessarily have the privilege of a good starting line but have taken advantage of the apparent inequality to develop necessary skills to make them what they are. In fact, it can some-times be to one's disadvantage to be blessed with a good starting line.

Babies, given who they are, would have mounted a huge protest to be rebirthed in the right location had they gotten the opportunity. In retrospect, I can see myself as having been born in the right place: in a village where there was no running water and no electricity. Disease-carrying insects, notably flies and mosquitoes ready to cause havoc, abounded. Frequent visitations from poi-sonous snakes were a common phenomenon. They strayed into human dwell-ings in search of food. Not uncommonly, huge crabs strolled in the pathways from the neighboring rivers. Chickens and goats roamed freely in human dwell-ings and sometimes competed with them for their food. A village, or better yet, a claimed jungle where wild animals sometimes strayed into the one and only street, bewildered, as if in protest against two-legged creatures, humans, usurping their habitat—this was my starting line, which I happily embraced.

A village was completely blindfolded to the outside world. There were no television sets. Occasional homes had a radio, but the emissions were mostly in a foreign language, English, which we did not understand.

There was no visual or auditory exposure to the outside world, yet our environment was accepted as completely normal. All my friends were commit-ted to the same experience. You did not miss what you did not have. We were very happy children. And we were in a perfect world.

I have a small scar on my left cheek inflicted on me during my infancy by a locally renowned herbalist. It was a conscious effort to scar my face for the rest of my life—either that or leave me to perish from an attack of convulsions.

Most childhood illnesses like malaria and the common cold manifested as fevers. These illnesses were not treated promptly and appropriately, and they usually resulted in high fevers. The fevers ended up causing convulsions, which resulted in loss of life from lack of oxygen to the brain. This was a very common phenomenon in the village. Many lives were lost because of this preventable scenario. The locals attributed the loss of life to bad spirits. They took away life that was not protected.

The herbalists had designed a remedy to prevent children from being taken away by bad spirits. They made incisions, usually on one's face, with a knife and rubbed in their secret protective potion. The resulting scar gave the child additional protection. The spirits were believed to spare the lives of scarred children. This sounds very outlandish, but it was the reality.

I was lucky to have a hardly noticeable scar. Perhaps I had a kindhearted herbalist. Some of the scars were really severe. I had many friends whose scars were on their bellies. These were children surviving the effects of sickle cell disease manifesting as swollen bellies. It was an attempt to cure them of this disease. Many Africans with such extensive scars on their bodies will have similar reasons for having them.

Imagine a world where toys are too expensive for parents to afford them. Yes, that was the case for me. That did not stop us. We made our own toys. We made dolls from clay and wood. We made cars from bamboo and the raffia plant.

We relied on friends to play, and toys were not a big deal in our lives. The society was very interconnected, and there appeared to be no boundaries. You played in any home or compound you wanted. You roamed freely with no fear of harm or kidnapping and reappeared in the house only when you were hungry.

The common notion is that childhood friends were the best and lasted forever. This was because of the time invested to make those friends. Relying on them for sharing ideas and exploring the harsh, unknown world consolidated those friendships. There was less reliance on technology, so there was more human interaction. Many people have cherished these friendships well into their adulthood.

In my case, as I write this memoir in my fifties, most of my childhood friends have perished, though not because they did anything wrong. They simply obeyed the laws of the land—living in the village where life expectancy was between fifty-five and sixty-five.

I have seen some of them succumbing to treatable diseases like tuberculosis, typhoid fever, and cholera, others to snake bites and natural phenomena like lightning. Some of the deaths were mysterious, sudden, and unexplained, and the person did not receive modern medical attention. One particular friend and his parents died in their sleep when their mud house collapsed on them. A couple of my childhood friends remaining in the village look very weathered and aged.

I would have been part of the statistics had I remained in the village. I thank God for the opportunity He gave to my parents to grant me a further education that allowed me the tailwind that propelled me into civilization.

Clothing was very simple. There were local tailors. Once a year, just before Christmas, your parents would take you to the market to choose a material you liked, or they would purchase one of their choice. Then they would send you to the tailor. He would take your measurements, and within a few days, your new clothes were ready. New clothes were usually donned on important occasions like Christmas or Easter and subsequently worn only on Sundays for church. The new clothes were complemented by a pair of new sandals.

On all other days of the week, it was not appropriate to be seen in new clothes and sandals. You were considered pompous and lazy. The norm was to be in tattered clothes and barefoot. The day-to-day clothes were bought from the local market, the *obroniwaawu* dealer. This translates to "clothing left behind by a dead Caucasian." These were imported, secondhand clothes. They sold at different prices, depending on how worn out they were. Depending on the pockets of your parents, you would be assigned one or two pairs. These you would wear for a very long time until they were completely worn out or you had grown out of them.

A bird's-eye view of our childhoods depicts how environmental factors modify our genetic expressions. Everyone is born with sets of genes designed to fully express themselves when the environment allows. The resulting adult size, shape, and constitution of humans are a combination of genes and environment. Clearly, my generation in the village has been shortchanged by the rule.

We were brought up in a farming village with an abundance of yams, coco yams, cassava, and plantains. These were mainly carbohydrates. Protein was usually from game and fish; these were relatively expensive. There was also the adult rule about nutrition, where the more senior you were, the better part of the meal you would be apportioned. So the expensive protein was disproportionally given to the adults, and children got very minimal. You would usually rush to clear your dad's table because there might be leftovers of fish or a chunk of meat.

What was obvious, therefore, was that growth was significantly affected by lack of protein and vitamins. There was an abundance of beriberi, a skin disease resulting from vitamin deficiency; kwashiorkor, a form of severe protein malnutrition; bowlegged kids; knocked knees; discolored hair; stunted growth; goiters; and many more conditions associated with nutritional deficiencies.

I had my fair share of nutritional deficiencies. I kept an Afro hairstyle, very bushy. It was discolored brown. Like other kids, I frequently dyed it to keep it black in color. Hair dyeing was a big business in the village. At the time, I did not know it was because of malnutrition.

I had a knock-knee problem when I was growing up, a condition associated with a vitamin deficiency where the legs curve toward each other at the knees. I was very conscious of it, and I tried to correct it by myself. For many years, I walked in a way that exerted outward pressure on my knees. This seemed to have straightened my leg.

I had a dry beriberi, another vitamin deficiency from which a rash appeared on my belly and legs. We usually scrubbed our bodies hard with a sharp sponge to even out the color.

Finally, I did not achieve my optimum height. At five feet ten inches, I am shorter than my dad, who was six feet tall, and my son, who was brought up in the United States and achieved his full genetic height of six feet two inches. I lacked the necessary nutrition during my adolescence that allowed the bones to grow a bit longer before they fused at the growth plate.

The objective of having many children in the village was to reap the benefits the family derived from the work the children provided to the household. Therefore, the prime objective of getting married was to produce children, and when the woman could not produce any children, the fault was mostly hers.

Children were produced at a rate determined by the body's natural family-planning system. Conception occurred only during the ovulation and fertilization window of three to four days in the cycle. And during breastfeeding, which was practiced across the board for at least two years, the hormonal changes did not allow pregnancy to occur again until breastfeeding was stopped.

There was no existence of family planning as we know it. It is amazing how this system allowed an average gap of two years between successive siblings.

Since we were part of the workforce, we had to work on the farm. This was mandatory. We were involved in all the farming activities, from clearing the bushes and manually tilling the land to planting, harvesting, storing, and carrying the crops on our heads to the market. During the school year, we went to the farm from five to eight in the morning, and after school, we went from four to dark, which was usually about six thirty in the evening.

We worked barefooted. We had many injuries. The multiple scars on my shins always remind me of the childhood labor. Now that I have become a doctor, I can attribute many of the mysterious deaths in the village to tetanus. These were clearly preventable deaths.

I almost drowned one time in my early years. I may have been eight or nine years old. This has left an indelible memory in my head to the extent that, to this day, I am unable to swim in a pool area where my feet cannot touch the ground.

It was in a big river that ran through the village, River Pompom. It is now a shadow of itself because of global warming. The river was the main source of fish in the village. The fishermen, with their canoes and dragnets, would catch huge quantities of tilapia and catfish. On Sundays, many kids would get their catches with fishhooks. In the rainy season, the river would overflow into the surrounding woods. Kids would be seen climbing the flooded trees and jumping into the water, and then they swam ashore. The river provided a good pastime activity for kids.

We were always warned by our parents not to swim in this river because we would drown. The disrespectful kids who did not heed their parents' cautions would always venture into the river, and gradually, by themselves, they learned how to swim. The good kids missed out on this thrill and became inexperienced in the river.

One afternoon, during the school lunch break, I accompanied some of my friends to the river. They were going to swim. I stood by the riverbank, watching them climb trees, hang on to the branches with one hand, and dive into the big river. Multiple times they did so effortlessly. It looked very easy from my point of view. Then I began salivating. Then one of them shouted, "Hey, come over; you can do it. Just jump and paddle your legs very fast." I did not hesitate.

I took off my clothes and—naked, of course—climbed one of the trees in the water, hung on its branch, and edged myself into the deeper end. Then, with pride and an amazing thrill from my onlooking friends, I let go of the branch and dropped into the water fast. I found myself at the bottom, paddling my legs fast like I was told.

To my great surprise, I was not resurfacing. I started sweating in the water. I was getting tired. I had my eyes closed, and my breath was getting short. It appeared I was under the water for a very long time.

Then I felt a push from below me. I came to the realization that I was sitting on the shoulder of one of the girls in the water. She had dived into the water to save my life. It was a near-death experience for me.

The story broke out in the school and in the village of the heroine who saved a boy's life. The topic of discussion was not a brave young girl but, as culture permitted, a very weak boy at the mercy of a girl. As one could imagine, other kids teased me for a very long time about this reversal of prowess.

To this day, I am very respectful of water depths, and swimming does not come naturally. I always have flashbacks of my near drowning, and I will always avoid going to the deep ends in swimming pools. Medically, psychotherapy and systematic desensitization would fix this problem.

When you ask a child or adolescent of modern times in urban areas what they would do for entertainment if they found themselves in a village with no modern technology like the Internet, Wi-Fi, television, electricity, or even running water, most of them may not be able to come up with answers.

The reality is that most of us found ourselves in this condition by virtue of our birth. I believe that this may be one of the reasons I have been equipped with the skill of creativity. All my life, I have been the first to do something different from the norm. I always look at a glass of water as half-full rather than half-empty. I always make the best of a bad situation.

In a remote village like Oterkpolu, the kids always found something to occupy themselves. During the daytime, we played soccer, jumped rope, and held running competitions. The running was on two legs, on legs and arms together, or on legs in sacks. We made our own soccer balls from the rubber trees we grew on our farms. The girls played ampey, a kind of jumping game in which the opponent would have to guess which foot the other party would put forward when landing from a jump.

We organized many soccer competitions with the surrounding villages. You can imagine that during the away matches, the visiting team would have to walk for miles to get to its destination. You would think the visiting team would always lose because of the disadvantage of the long walk, but this was not usually the case.

During the night, which was usually dark everywhere, we gathered around the kerosene lamp either at home or at a neighbor's house and told or listened to *ananse* stories. These were fairy tales regarding spiders. These stories were narrated by renowned storytellers, usually the elders, who passed on their skills to the youth.

The physical activity of the youth, seemingly imposed on them by circumstances beyond their control, exerted a great and beneficial impact on their adult physical structures. Medical fact has it that all humans are born with weak bones, which gradually harden to a maximum density at age eighteen. Then the density remains static until age thirty-five. After that, the bone begins to lose its density until you perish. To achieve the maximum bone strength requires a lot of physical activity during the period when the bone is hardening. Therefore, the bone strength you attain at age eighteen is the one you will have for the rest of your life. Weaker bones at eighteen years certainly lead to adulthood osteoporosis and fractures. In retrospect, I can now explain why there were hardly anyone in the village with broken bones.

Other forms of entertainment in the village were live bands, magic shows, and dramas. Dancing and singing came naturally to the villagers. My worst talent, though, was singing.

There were no age restrictions on alcohol or tobacco use; however, these habits were stigmatized as belonging to those with bad upbringings. Indulgence in such activities was limited to grown-ups or those who were able to look after themselves.

Life was not boring as a growing child in the village. There was plenty of activity and fun. We were happy. The most important thing was taking what was available to us at the time and making the best out of it. As we silently acquired these skills, we integrated them into the fabric of our making. Then we put them to good use to navigate a world that has an abundance of opportunities apparent only to the initiated.

Chapter 5

THE EDUCATIONAL SYSTEM IN GHANA

Ghana, being a British colony, acquired its educational system from Great Britain. It had a three-tier system of education.

There was a basic elementary education comprising a primary school of six years, starting at age six, followed by four years of a middle school. You graduated the middle school with a middle school leaving certificate. This certificate was good for menial jobs in the factory, the police force, the military, and so on.

The secondary education was composed of a five-year general education followed by a two-year sixth-form education. Admission into the five-year phase was dependent on successfully passing an exam while in the middle school. This was the common entrance exam. Success in this exam opened the way for a secondary education, if only your family could afford it. A general certificate of education (GCE) ordinary level was awarded at the end of the five years.

Then the two-year sixth-form education prepared you for your career; you focused on three core subjects. Admission was dependent on one's performance on the GCE ordinary level. At the end of the two-year sixth-form education, you were awarded a GCE advanced level. Then came the university education. Performance at the GCE advanced level determined which career path you pursued.

Education was free in Ghana except for the five-year secondary education. This bottleneck deselected many good students in the middle school whose parents could not afford the secondary school. Furthermore, the higher levels of education had very limited positions, and it was by design to select the best students.

Many students who were not fortunate enough to make it to the mainstream of education, as a result of either financial or academic deficiency, got enrolled into the polytechnics and teacher training to learn careers like plumbing, electrical, secretarial, teaching, and so on.

The educational structure, based on the British system, did not address the needs of the wider population, especially villages like mine. It was at variance with the socioeconomic structure of the country and has doomed the lives of many villagers. Some of these people were better than me but, paradoxically, held back by an institution designed to help them.

However, candidates who have been successfully milled through the system are able to face the world wherever they find themselves. While I am thankful for having gone through such a system, I am very aware of the less fortunate who could not make it for one reason or the other.

Chapter 6

ELEMENTARY EDUCATION

As expected, I was very eager to start my first grade in school, class one. As it was the norm to show maturity to enter class one, I was constantly testing my reach to the opposite ear with one arm over my head. When I finally did it, I knew I was six years old and quickly got enrolled the following school year.

The only teacher whose name I can remember as I write this memoir is Miss Ankrah. She was my class-one teacher. Her name has stuck in my head all these years because of the constant flashbacks of my class-one experience.

First there is an enjoyable flashback. The class appeared easy. It was simply assigning English names to common objects and doing simple addition and subtraction, which we performed in our local language. With *My First Copy Book*, we copied the alphabet, which at the time felt like we were drawing the letters, and distinguished between small and capital letters. During class playtimes, we would sit on the ground under the trees with Miss Ankrah. Then she would tell us sweet stories or introduce us to various group games. We played hide-and-seek and a board game called *oware*. We sang children's songs and danced. My introductory education was joyful and served as a magnet that propelled me into the kingdom of academia.

Then there is the traumatizing flashback of learning to spell my name, John. For some reason, Miss Ankrah expected me to be able to spell my name correctly. She was surprised that I could not spell it. I tried various sound combinations of John. When I failed to come up with the correct spelling, Miss Ankrah detained me in the class during the lunch period. I was so ashamed. While in detention, the kids would pass by the window, some to make fun of me and a few others to help by whispering the spelling to me. Try as they might, the whisperings were not clear enough to make me get the right spelling.

Finally, the one-hour break was over. I did not have lunch. Class resumed. I still was not able to spell my name. Miss Ankrah asked who could spell my name. One boy in class, Teye, raised his hand and spelled it. At first the spelling looked weird to me, but gradually it began to look right.

Teye became my best friend. He was a very intelligent boy. He had a very distinctive feature that made him stand out from the rest of the kids. His head shape looked different from the rest of us. It was rectangular. It was as if the skull had been placed in a rectangular box while it was hardening. As a result, children nicknamed him January-to-December, representing his long head.

The nickname did not perturb him. For the first four years of primary school, January-to-December was always at the top of the class, followed by a girl called Larkwor. Then I came in third position. There were about fifteen to twenty kids in each class.

The educational system then was such that at the end of every trimester, there was an exam. Then all the students were graded and arranged in order of performance. On the last day of the trimester, which happened three times a year, all the kids would line up according to their class. Then the headmaster would announce the exam grading of each class, going from the best student to the worst. You were noticeable if you were the best or the worst student.

The primary school was very basic. It was made up of two sets of buildings facing each other. They stood about one hundred meters apart. The space between the two buildings was covered with patchy, uneven grass and shrubs, crisscrossed by paths of denuded ground created by neighboring inhabitants walking innocently across the school compound to perform their daily chores. One of the buildings was divided into three smaller rooms that were linked by a common veranda. This represented classes one to three. The second building was divided into four rooms, also with a common veranda. This represented classes four to six and the headmaster's office.

Then there was a good-size soccer field stretching across one end of the two buildings. Large leftover trees peppered the surrounding vicinity, providing shade and shelter from the unrelenting tropical sun and doubling as playgrounds for the pupils.

The school was considered upscale by virtue of being a Roman Catholic school, which were reputed to have more details in their buildings' structures. It was constructed with cement blocks and plastered with cement mortar. Patchy and peeling white calico paint finish on walls represented a school that had outlived its past glories. There was a representation of large windows and doors, but these were never fitted. The floors were concrete. There was no electricity, and there were no fans. Each classroom was fitted with a blackboard. A small stand near the blackboard was fashioned to place white chalk and a duster on it.

From class one to class three, each pupil brought his or her own table and chair. We left them in the classroom during the trimester but took them home during the long breaks. As there were no secured doors or windows, some of this furniture would occasionally go walking, and the pupil would be forced to attend classes sitting on the floor until a parent could afford to replace it.

From class one to class three, each pupil was assigned a small writing blackboard, about one foot square in size. We called it a slate. With the slate and a piece of white chalk, we did our sums and practiced how to write.

From class four to class six, we were provided with furniture purchased by the school. These were chunky, ugly desks that sat two pupils and reminded me of the old-fashioned long pews in the church. At this level of education, we graduated from using chalk and slates to exercise books, pencils, and erasers.

The middle school was located half a mile from the primary school. This appeared newer. It shared a compound with the only fanciful Catholic church in the locality. The school consisted of one block of a partially completed building divided into four rooms with a veranda, representing forms one to four. The walls were not plastered with cement mortar and showed a block-work arrangement evident of a contribution from locally volunteered unskilled labor. The floors were cemented. The headmaster's office was located in the sacristy of the church building.

There were no janitors. The pupils' responsibility was to clean the class-rooms of the surrounding compound. This duty was usually performed during the first half hour of school.

The students kept the weeds and shrubs in the school compound under control. Each class was assigned a portion of the compound. When the weeds overgrew, the teacher would set a day and ask all the students to bring cutlasses. That day would be the weeding day; there would be no classes until the work was over.

Gradually we moved through the grades. Like all kids, you learn to read and then you read to learn. This was easier said than done. Learning English was very difficult. It was not spoken anywhere in the village. The only time we heard anyone speaking English was in the school, either from teachers or from visiting expatriate Roman Catholic priests. We memorized words and spellings and phrases. Putting them together in sentences was way out of reach of any pupil. So it was considered a school practice, and we were very happy to speak our own language at home.

I found arithmetic very refreshing to learn. I remember it being full of colorful diagrams of mangoes and bananas in various combinations, pictorially teaching us how to count, add, subtract, and divide. I can still smell the new arithmetic workbooks that got progressively harder as we went through the echelons of the school system.

Our English comprehension was very limited in the primary school, and subjects were taught through a combination of English and the local language. We studied nature and sanitation in the early years. As our English developed in senior years, we were introduced to children's books. I remember the cartoons describing the lines of sentences underneath.

Graduating to the middle school was more exciting. We were now reading to learn. In addition to English and mathematics, we studied history, science, geography, and arts. Instead of pencils, we were required to write in pens. This left no room for mistakes. You could not erase a word wrongly spelled. You gathered your thoughts before writing. Poorly organized students stood out. The good students always had clean work.

All the pupils wore a uniform provided by their families. This consisted of a beige khaki shirt and a pair of khaki shorts. Usually one uniform was provided per child, which we wore until it was worn out or we grew too big for it. We wore this uniform five days a week. On Saturdays, we hand-washed them and starched them. Then they were allowed to dry in the plentiful sunshine and fresh air. On Sundays, children would iron their own uniforms with a hot iron. The hot iron consisted of a triangular iron box containing a burning charcoal.

January-to-December was in his element in school, rapidly gaining popularity with his academic ability and distinctive head shape. He collected all the school prizes for the first four years of primary school. He would rattle off the alphabet and numbers, rapidly perform additions and subtractions, and then do multiplications and divisions with automatic alacrity. He was like a calculating machine.

He was an exemplary pupil, and the teachers loved him. My liking for his academic prowess attracted me to him immediately. Soon we became very close friends. In line with the Montessori principle of education, where children of various age groups and abilities are put together in one class, I began to copy his traits. We were inseparable both at school and outside school.

With January-to-December now as my mentor, I began to challenge myself. By class three, I was second in the class, overtaking the number-two girl, Larkwor. I really liked school now.

From class four onward, English words in sentences began to make sense. I became an avid reader. But there was no library in the school or in the village. The only available books were kept on shelves in the headmaster's office. We read them during school time, and they were taken away from us when school was over.

January-to-December and I had to fashion a plan of getting some of these books home on the blind side of the teachers. We would devise various plans to distract the teachers then sneak books under our shirts. We even ventured into the headmaster's office once when he was teaching a class and made away with some books.

The irony was that we were caught once when we were returning some of the books to class. It was obvious the books had been well read, evidenced by the palm-oil stains transferred from our improperly washed hands after eating.

Discipline in schools was very strict. Mischief like this in a school was punishable by caning. So January-to-December and I received a few lashes for trying to challenge our abilities.

By the third trimester of class five, and for the first time ever, I came out on top of the class exam, overtaking January-to-December. This created a big uproar not only in the school but also in the village. I felt other kids started looking at me differently, probably with respect for beating the number-one well-known icon.

From this time onward and throughout middle school, there was no looking back for me. I consistently maintained my lead in class until one semester in form two in the middle school. A new schoolteacher joined the middle school. She brought with her a daughter of our age. She was called Grace. For one trimester in form two, because of my complacency, Grace beat me to a second position. It caused a bit of an upset, but I quickly recovered.

January-to-December was still my friend in middle school. With his aid, I tried to impress the other kids by performing multiple magical illusions I had picked up from my magician brother. We cheated other kids during card games. He would stand behind my opponent, read his card, and tell me all the cards with predetermined eye and finger signs.

So far, school was good. During form two, as was the practice, the teachers would select the best students to take the common entrance examination, the examination that qualified us to proceed to the next level of education, a secondary school. Five of us were selected, including Grace and January-to-December. Out of the five, only four of us passed. This included Grace, January-to-December, and me. However, out of the four of us who had passed this rate-determining examination, I was the only one whose parents could afford to financially support a secondary education.

It was now time for me to part with January-to-December. I moved out of the village to the boarding school. January-to-December stayed on in the middle school and graduated with a middle school leaving certificate. As his parents were not able to afford even a vocational training like carpentry, January-to-December had no other choice than to become a farmer from his teens. He farmed any crop that would make him money, from tobacco, plantain, cassava, and corn to even marijuana.

I visited the village during school vacations. We played soccer together; we shared ideas and his frustrations about how he was missing out on secondary education. He filled me in on all the gossip from my absence. He got married in his twenties like one would expect. He had multiple kids as was the tradition. He was living the normal village life.

The dichotomy in our paths really took a toll on January-to-December. He aged very rapidly from the hard manual labor in the scorching tropical sun. As if he were one of the old folks in the village, I saw him losing one tooth after the other, darkening and wrinkling, and progressively looking older and older than his age. In later years, when I was financially comfortable, I would drive my car to the village. He would come to me, and all he would do was weep as if to say that he would have had similar comfort if he had had the opportunity of getting a secondary education. I would comfort him and give him some money.

Sadly, in accord with the proven statistics of life expectancy in the village—between fifty-five and sixty-five years—January-to-December died in his late forties as a very poor man after a short illness. The villagers considered him an old man; his kids, who were also unfortunate to be snowballed into a pecuniary challenge, stalled after their middle school education as well. They lacked the means to bury him. At this time, I was in a very comfortable position, and I showed my last respect by easing the financial burden of his family.

I frequently reflect on the life of my best childhood friend, January-to-December. At the time of writing this chronicle, I have achieved most of my life's dreams and am passing the baton to my kids so they do not have to commence from the starting line, whereas the progeny of January-to-December are still entangled in the secluded world in the village, unable to make any headway from the starting line because of circumstances beyond their control.

Chapter 7

SECONDARY EDUCATION

I started my secondary education at the age of fifteen. Two careers were predetermined for me by my parents. Mom wanted me to become a policeman, and Dad wanted me to be a Roman Catholic priest. But my secret dream was to become an ambassador so I could travel around the world.

I was set up to start a secondary education. Like with all other students, my parents provided me with a trunk and a chop box. The trunk was a metal case that was characteristically painted black with scattered yellow stars or circles. It contained my clothes. The chop box was a wooden box made from plywood and odum and fitted with a padlock. It was a mini grocery shop containing milk, sugar, soaps, and instant dry food, notably the ever-popular *gari* made from cassava. It was supposed to supplement the meager food served in the boarding house and mitigate the hunger between school meals.

The secondary school was located in the regional capital, called Koforidua. It was a Roman Catholic school, Pope John Secondary School, and was only for boys. Coming from the village, I saw it as a magnificent setup. It had running water and electricity. It was confined within a larger area with clear boundaries made up of a combination of forest in certain areas and barbed wire. There were only two official entrances to the school.

It had multiple buildings that were able to accommodate three classrooms per each of the five-year academic courses. A large science laboratory block stood in one corner. There was an impressive Catholic church at the other corner and a residence to house all the priests, who also doubled as teachers. Then, about two hundred meters away from the main school blocks were the dormitory buildings. One of these buildings was clearly labeled "Seminary House."

The seminary house was where I was settled because of my predetermined career. It was a dormitory supposed to house students who would become Catholic priests. Many of them did. As expected, the students were supposed to lead exemplary lives and be pious and kind. This was also evident in many of the students I met. About twenty students shared a room and slept on noisy metal bunk beds. I was assigned the bottom bunk, where I settled in with my trunk and chop box.

The school admitted students from all over the country. It had a very high academic standard, and the admitting criteria were based on good grades from the common entrance exam in the middle school and being a Roman Catholic.

This system of secondary education, designed by the first president of Ghana, Dr. Kwame Nkrumah, served a very important purpose for Ghana: prevention of tribal wars. It is almost impossible to wage a tribal war in Ghana. The secondary school was a melting pot where any kid, irrespective of tribe, was admitted. From a very early age, we mingled and befriended people from all over the country. The unintended consequence for me was rapid improvement of spoken English. Suddenly, in the boarding school, we found ourselves with other students who spoke the many different Ghanaian languages. The only common form of communication was English.

There existed an unofficial initiation process for all freshmen in the secondary and tertiary schools. This process was called *homo*. During this process, the senior students subjected the freshmen to many physical and psychological abuses during the first few weeks of the school year. It was fun for the senior students but very traumatic to the freshmen. In my case, my abuser was a senior student in my dormitory. He slapped my face one afternoon after school and then forced open my chop box and took my meager supply of groceries. Frustrated and helpless, I reported him to the housemaster, Mr. Narh. He was summoned, suspended, and removed from the seminary house. It was clear that he did not fit the characteristics of a future priest.

Life in the Catholic boarding school was very regimented and put a structure in my and the other kids' lives that has stayed with me to this day. The typical school day started at five o'clock in the morning. Students had one hour to have a shower, dress, make their beds, and be in church—compulsory for seminarians—at six o'clock in the morning. The morning mass usually lasted less than one hour, depending on the priest. At seven o'clock, breakfast was served in a huge dining hall. Twelve students were assigned to each table. Then classes began at eight o'clock in the morning and lasted until two o'clock in the afternoon, followed by a short lunch break and a siesta from two to four. Dinner was served at 6:00 p.m. From seven to nine, there was a supervised private study in the classroom. By 9:15 p.m., all students had to be in bed, and lights-out and roll call were at nine thirty.

Each student was allowed about four passes on Saturdays to go out into the city, usually to look around and replenish the mini grocery store. Parents were allowed to visit about once a month.

I was eager to be in the classroom with other kids from all over the country. I quickly made new friends to replace January-to-December. The school was well staffed with a diverse mix of teachers from around the world, notably France, England, and the United States. There were few female teachers. The priest contributed immensely to the teaching of literature and religion. In addition to the staff, the school was equipped with all I needed. This was my perfect storm and my springboard that catapulted me into academia and enabled me to go places I would never have imagined, meeting people from all over the world and humbly looking back to my roots and saying, "I did it." It was a time that taught me that what matters most is not where one comes from but where one is going.

I was a good student—dedicated, conscientious—and it soon became obvious to the teachers that I did not come to play; however, there were a few challenges with my school fees during the first year. There were three terms per school year. During the second and third terms, it became apparent to me that my parents were struggling to come up with the school fees when it was time for me to go back to school. There was nothing I could do other than put in my maximum effort in the farmwork during the school holidays and hope that everything went fine.

Then, during the long vacation between the first and second years, my school report arrived. My parents, being illiterates, would not understand it, so I had to translate my performance to them in the local language. The first page was the report itself. The second page was the invoice for the fees for the next term, which they dreaded. Then a third page was a letter from the scholarship board. This letter explained that as a result of my exceptional performance, I had been awarded a government scholarship for the remaining four years to cover my tuition and boarding starting from the first term of the next academic year. As one could imagine, my heart leaped, and my parents burst into tears of joy.

In the spell of the moment, thoughts quickly ran through my mind that I should interpret the letter from the scholarship board to mean that the scholarship would start from the second term. That did not change their joy because they did not know otherwise. The rationale was to use the first term school fees they would give me to start a business to help defray the cost of my sibling, who was also starting his secondary education that same year. Indeed, with the fees of the first term, I bought myself a used black-and-white camera, and I was set to start my first business, which will be elaborated on in the chapter about business ventures.

Now that financial impediment was no longer an excuse, I was on a cruising trajectory, and the sky was the limit. My only enemy was myself. I was the only one who could spoil it for me. I did not want to disappoint myself, and my dedication to books was second to none. I was awarded many achievement prizes in multiple subjects over the remaining four years. My elder brother's influence urged me to work harder in French, and by the end of the second year, I was the only student to speak French and the best in that subject in the history of the school. I was fascinated by Latin, and even though most students deemed it a dead language, I perfected the nuances in that subject as if it were my mother tongue. I loved all subjects, but my effortless strength was in mathematics and the sciences. I hated physical education, music, and the local Ghanaian language, Twi.

All was going in my favor except for a couple of students in the class who posed a threat to me. They were also very good students. We challenged one another in the class, and sometimes they scored better than me. I did not like that.

One of the students in my class gossiped that my challengers had a charm that helped enhance their memories. I became very interested, and I asked my friend where I could go for that charm.

A few weeks later, during the third year of secondary education, I got a Saturday pass and went to the city with my friend to a malam, the Muslim version of the juju man. He asked me to bring certain items, including the shell of a tortoise. With the powdered tortoise shell, he added his secret concoction. He asked me to take it to school with clear instructions on how to drink it.

I was happy and ready to challenge those students who were posing the intellectual problems. I kept the concoction in my chop box. I took the first drink and then the second drink the following day. This daily potion was supposed to continue for two weeks. By the third day, the effect was noticeable, sweet but unpleasant, and I had to give it up.

For two straight weeks, I had so much physical and mental energy and was so wide awake that I could not sleep. I suddenly became a fast reader. I would normally take one week to read a storybook, but now it took me only one day. The undesirable and disappointing effect was that I did not retain anything I read, and I became very fatigued. For the period of two weeks, I performed very poorly in class and was very disappointed with myself. I cursed the friend who had introduced me to the malam.

At the end of the two weeks, I suffered a weird attack that landed me in the hospital.

My heart was racing, the muscles in my belly contracted, and I was folded over and walking as if someone were sitting on my shoulders and another person was pushing me from behind. I was suffering from great exhaustion. I was hospitalized for a week. I was given some medication that slowed down my heartbeat and then intravenous fluids and other medications. I never disclosed what I took, nor was I asked.

The doctor who took care of me was so cool, calm, and gentle that I immediately had admiration for him. At that moment, a career as a doctor came into my head. I wanted to be like him. I asked his name, and in a gentle voice, he replied, "Dr. John Appiah." He was a very young graduate from the only medical school, and that was his first posting in the Catholic hospital. To this day we are very good friends.

I was discharged back to school, learning a great lesson from this near-death experience. I quietly emptied my chop box of the noxious concoction and cursed my soul, saying that I would never do such a thing again. In life, there are challenges for a reason. Better students are always planted there to urge weaker ones to do better, just like the decoys we see in the Olympic track competition.

The message of learning to be oneself and not wishing you were someone else can come in many forms. Another form it took for me, and what drove this message home, was when I wished I had been born into the families of the rich kids in school. Some of them were the kids of the then military rulers and their cronies in Ghana. Those kids came to school with the latest fashion, shoes, and so on. The first time I heard about Adidas was when a friend brought to my attention that one of those kids was wearing a pair of Adidas sneakers. I was not impressed because I did not know what the brand Adidas was. Before long, there came a popular military uprising in Ghana, headed by Jerry John Rawlings, to end the reign of the then corrupt government. The parents of some of those kids fled the country, and others were executed. The school fashion show was over, and the reality check was that I did not want to be anyone other than me and should not get carried away with what someone else has.

At the end of the third year, students were required to have a one-on-one meeting with the career counseling board to decide whether to pursue arts or science for the remaining two years. I was faced with my predetermined parental careers of being a policeman or a priest and my newly acquired epiphany. After easily eliminating a policeman career, I wanted to be both a doctor and a priest. I was made aware that these two careers were mutually incompatible at the same time and that I could become a priest later after completing medical school. So my journey was defined and crystallized.

My last two years were dedicated to science, French, and geography. I was committed to using my natural ability to be the best.

Then came the national general certificate of examination ordinary level exams. My hard work paid off. Not only did I beat all the students in my class, but I was the best student in the whole country on this exam.

At that moment, I wished my parents were literates so they could understand the gravity of my success and share my happiness. My father eventually came to the realization when he was walking from the farm one day. One of our teachers, a Catholic priest, Father Batsa, was driving to the village for a church activity. Father Batsa stopped and gave my dad a ride home. My father said this was different for the priest to stop, pick him up, and drive him home. The conversation during the short ride was about me. The priest explained to him what I did and its impact on my future and congratulated him for giving me the opportunity. That was the moment my father became very impressed with my performance.

Following this success, I gained entry into the best science college in Ghana, Presbyterian Boys Secondary School, for the two-year sixth-form education. There I studied the three core subjects in science: chemistry, physics, and biology. The school had the best of everything.

I made new friends there. As one can imagine, each of them was the cream of the crop. We challenged one another, we studied together, and each one of them knew his future career was set, either in engineering or medicine. We were not competing against one another. We were competing to gain admission to the limited positions in the universities to pursue our respective careers.

The only challenge I experienced in this boarding school was hunger. The school was located in the capital city of Ghana, Accra, approximately one hundred miles from the village. The distance was coupled with the severe pecuniary challenges facing my parents; they were unable to provide money or food to supplement the meager meals provided in the boarding house. I adapted to functioning with very little food. I remember suffering from lots of headaches and migraines during this period, and surely this was from low blood sugar.

But the end justified the means. After two years of devoted study, I passed the general certificate of examination advanced level with extreme ease in 1981.

At the interview for the medical school, which had positions for only fifty students per year, we were all lined up according to our performance in the advanced-level examination. In that line, the first forty would surely gain admission based on merit and the additional ten for other reasons. I was number one in the line. I was now set to be a doctor.

Chapter 8

UNIVERSITY EDUCATION

y six-year medical training started in 1981. A class of the fifty best students drawn from all over the country, we were the elite in what was then the only medical school in Ghana. The medical school was free at the time, and my parents, who had very limited financial resources, did not have to come up with any money. The village boy from Oterkpolu had graduated from living in dormitories to a single room, all by himself, at Akuafo Hall at the University of Ghana's main campus in Legon. It was the final assurance that financial independence was only six years away.

The medical education was very challenging. There was a lot of reading and memorization, and as my intellect was made for this, I found it rather interesting and wanted more. I was impressed by how the Almighty God put together a perfect animal chemistry at the microscopic level and how a synchronized functioning of all these chemicals allowed us to talk, walk, eat, breathe, think, and combat one another—so mundane that we take it all for granted. I was intrigued by how diseases arise by interruption of this perfect system and how to identify the insulting agent and deal with it in a designed manner. I could never see myself studying any subject other than medicine.

The real challenge came to me in anatomy class. I did not realize we would be intimately dealing with dead bodies. First we were all given wooden boxes. When I opened mine, it contained all the bones in the human body. We were to take it home and return them at the end of the anatomy year. It was different sleeping in the same room with a skeleton. The day after sleeping with the skeleton, we were asked to interact with the real thing. The anatomy laboratory opened, and all I could smell was the pungent odor of formalin, the embalming chemical used to preserve cadavers. Then I saw motionless humans respectfully arranged on terrazzo tables all over the laboratory. Surrounding us behind locked glass cabinets were various human parts carefully sliced and labeled.

We all stopped in our tracks after seeing this. Then I heard the professor shout, "Come in, come in." In our little white coats, I could feel the shock on everyone's face. Two students were assigned to one cadaver, who was introduced to us with a name. We were asked to use his name anytime we made reference to him, just as you would do with a living person. He had been a mentally ill patient abandoned by his family in the hospital after his demise.

Then we were given a dissection book and a scalpel box. Following the instructions from the book, and for one year, we dissected the cadaver from the shoulder to the toes. We studied all the bones, muscles, blood vessels, nerves, eyes, the brain, and all the internal organs. By the end of the year, the whole cadaver had disappeared piecemeal.

During the clinical years, it became apparent to me that I did not like blood. This was during my obstetrics training. Under supervision, each student was required to deliver a certain number of babies. Then we were required to manage the afterbirth problems. These included removal of the placenta and making sure it all came out and repairing the torn birth canal by suturing it together. Clearly this was bloody work. My soul could not stand the feeling of the crunchy placenta and the sight of blood clots. But I had no choice. Just like in life, you meet so many things that you do not like to do. But if you let the ego ride you, it will cost you a lot more.

I enjoyed pediatric medicine. My first impression was how you could tell what was wrong with a child when he or she did not speak. But after going through the motions of logic/science, it became very easy to make a diagnosis of a sick child. Children get sick very quickly, but when you make the right diagnosis in a timely manner, they heal very rapidly. I did not take children's medicine as a career because I find them too delicate and fragile, and seeing some of them having incurable diseases and cancers and enduring the wrath of chemotherapy would break my heart.

A doctor is trained to allow empathy to override sympathy, to show sincere concern but not attach. Such dissociation allows doctors to stay levelheaded when deciding what is best for patients. Doctors will not cry and wail when they lose a patient. In my case, with children's medicine, I do not know how good I would be.

Internal medicine is a perfect fit for me. It involves the intellectual ability to decipher what is wrong with patients just by talking to them, shaking hands with them, or hugging them. It was rumored that a famous physician in England was able to make a diagnosis of emphysema in a Russian president just by hugging him. According to the story, the president's barrel chest and being a smoker clinched the diagnosis. This is how internal medicine works.

Internal medicine is real intellectual academia. It requires a lot of detailed knowledge of how the various disease processes manifest in humans so that by looking at a person walk, hearing him or her speak, or looking at their hands and feet, the trained clinician can guess what is wrong even before talking to the patient. This requires a lot of training and experience, and mastery of this is the art of a good clinician. This was my best subject in medical school and the path I have chosen to pursue.

My worst subject was public health medicine. Even though it is an important branch of medicine, my preconceived idea of a doctor is someone who heals a sick person. Public health medicine is designed to study disease patterns in the community and design means to prevent it from spreading. I had to pass the subject to graduate. The trauma of this subject still follows me to this day. At least twice a year, I wake up with nightmares that the final examination in this subject is fast approaching and I have not prepared. It is the same dream over and over.

Medical school training was a big challenge, and over the ensuing six years, I witnessed thrill, drama, and tragedy. Nothing comes easily, and if you accept that premise, then you will never be disappointed by the bumps in the road.

Ghana Medical School, being the only one at the time in the country, held a very high international standard. It admitted only the best fifty students per year. To maintain the set standard, the examinations were designed to fail at least 10 percent of the students every year. When a student failed the exam, he or she was given one chance to rewrite the examination after six weeks. After failure to pass the second time, the student would be asked to repeat the year.

This standard put a lot of pressure on the students. Luckily, I never failed any examination in the medical school; however, I have seen students who have repeated multiple classes and completed their training beyond the stipulated six years.

Other students developed severe psychological stress and gave up the training. I have known some who took to illicit drug use and attempted suicide. I have also witnessed a few more who were actually brave enough to subject themselves to that final blow: a completed suicide.

My huge problem was student poverty. I was very poor. There was hardly any support from my parents because they could not afford it. By the third year, my mother kept telling me the course was getting too long and asking when I would finish looking after them. I supplemented my food with the help of good friends from richer homes. I give credit to Ashkar, a Lebanese classmate from a very rich home, who understood my predicament. I give credit also to my best friend, Jimmy Ray, a product of a rich Ashanti cocoa farmer. I was originally attracted to these two, who later became close friends, because of their tremendous delta force brainpower, able to assimilate gigantic amounts of information and regurgitate it with effortless automaticity.

I befriended a distant relative who worked in the pharmacy of the teaching hospital. She gave me the weekly disposed of, wasted vitamins; they were either crumbled or powdered. But when I went through the chaff, I would find a few whole tablets. I was able to harvest the whole tablets from the chaff. Then, once a month, I would travel to the village and sell it to the local drugstore. I would give some of the proceeds to my mother and keep the rest.

The extent of my poverty was such that I wore the same pair of black shoes over and over until the heels wedged and my bare big toe went through the sole. Then I would put a new sole on it at the cobbler and wear it over again. One time I took my ego so low that I asked one of my mates, who had many shoes, to give me one of his pairs. It was shameful enough to ask, but when he said no, it was even more devastating.

To make matters worse, the student body got involved in politics. This prolonged our already long course from six to seven years. The second military uprising, again led by Flight Lieutenant Jerry John Rawlings, was received with mixed feelings. During our second year of medical school, we, the student body of all three universities in Ghana, headed by its charismatic president, Arthur Kennedy, also a medical student, demanded the military government hand over power to a civilian government. We gave the military government an ultimatum, after which we would boycott lectures. When military rulers did not heed to our demand, we enforced our threat. After about two weeks of no lectures, the military government closed down all three universities for one year. Details of what ensued are beyond the scope of this book. But in brief, the student leader was captured and tortured, and eventually he escaped from the country.

During the hardship in medical school, I was unexpectedly rewarded by a patient's family. At the time, it was the reward I needed most. It was my first experience of how a good work could lead to good returns. This happened during my junior surgical clerkship. In our mini white coats with cheap Chinese stethoscopes around our necks, we were curious and enjoying our first exposure to surgery. During a night call, I was assigned a female patient who presented with acute appendicitis. She had had emergency surgery that night. It was my job to follow her and present her progress to my superiors, which I did with keen interest. In addition, I was also responsible for communicating her progress to her family. Her husband was Mr. Kapoor, an Indian businessman. Everything went according to plan, and she was discharged. In appreciation of the good outcome, Kapoor invited me to his house for dinner. What surprised me was that I was not even the surgeon; I was just the communicator.

Mr. Kapoor expressed his appreciation and rewarded me with clothes and money. This was the needed necessity in my life at the time. And he said that anytime I needed help, I should contact him.

Sadly, my dad passed away in my fourth year of medical school. The little moral and financial support I had suddenly disappeared. Worst of all, there was no money for his burial. I took it upon myself to find the money to give him his final dignity. That was when a friend of mine who was a medical officer in the teaching hospital came to my aid.

Trying to survive the final two years in medical school was the key that turned into the business career that was already inherent in me. It turned this misfortune into a big blessing. From this point onward, I have always worn two heads, the one that thinks like a doctor and the one that is entrepreneurial. I will elaborate on the details of how I made money during my final two years of medical school that made me a rich intern in the chapter about business ventures.

At the time, it was hard to afford the basic life necessities to subsist. I was faced with a curriculum requirement of externship soon after losing my dad. This was part of the medical training in the clinical years when students acquired experience from other teaching hospitals. It was required but not mandatory as the school was aware of the financial constraints of the students. Since there was no other medical institution in Ghana at the time, most able students acquired this experience in a hospital in London. I was able to secure a position for this externship at Chase Farm Hospital in Edmonton, London.

The only problem I was faced with was the money to pay for air tickets, a room, and food. As was the norm, I sought financial assistance from charity organizations like the rotary club and business institutions, but all proved futile. Then I thought of Mr. Kapoor. I told him I did not want a gift, but I wanted a loan. This impressed him. He asked for a guarantor. I was able to persuade my distant uncle Nii Armah to agree to be my guarantor. Nii Armah had a great deceiving personality; on the surface, he appeared rich and was always in likable, high spirits. He worked for an airline, the old British Caledonian, now British Airways. God bless Nii Armah's soul; he had empty pockets.

Uncle Nii Armah secured a milestone in my life's journey. Going to London for the first time opened many doors for me. The culture shock of seeing what was across the seas reignited my inner spirit.

I spent two out of the six weeks required in the teaching hospital in London for a surgery rotation. For the remaining four weeks, I had to work to pay back Mr. Kapoor.

I worked in a McDonald's restaurant backstage. Uniformed and complemented with their trademark baseball hat, I was assigned to make the beef burgers. I asked for any shift that was ever available. I worked the night shift to do the cleaning of the equipment and prepare for the morning breakfast. I worked almost every day of the week. I may have worked over twenty hours a day.

Four weeks later, I made enough money. I bought some clothes to appease my soul. The rest of the money was seed money for my business ventures, which I will elaborate on in the chapter about that subject. I was able to pay off Mr. Kapoor with proceeds from the business and bought him a nice gift from London.

With all of life's difficulties that I was presented with, I likened myself to Uncle Nii Armah, who could make good things happen with his personality and words. Feeling sympathy for oneself is a failure in life, whatever the circumstances. In fact, it was a good thrill for me to be swimming against the waves, and I really enjoyed it. We made life in medical school great fun. We followed the American movie stars and musical artists. We went to discos. We mingled and hobnobbed with the student nurses.

Being a Michael Jackson fan, I was fascinated by his mannerisms. I imitated his dancing to almost perfection. I even imitated his dressing style. I kept a very bushy Afro hairstyle. I wore trousers that stopped far above my ankles, complemented by a pair of white socks.

Attending lectures dressed like Michael Jackson did not go down well with faculty. I was falling out of the norm of expectations for a doctor. It was particularly offensive to the pediatric professor, Dr. Arthur. One can imagine how stressful it was to fall out of favor of a highly respected professor, revered for his intellectual ability, and pass through his department with success.

During the peak of my financial problems, I suffered a small setback. For the first time in my life, I failed one of the many clinical interim assessment examinations. Even though this did not have any impact on my final examination, I first tasted examination failure. The reason for this failure was that I did not have a wristwatch. In the course of the examination, the invigilator warned the class that the clock in the examination room was not functioning. Not having a wristwatch, I did not pace myself, and I did not finish the paper when time was up. Failure is a good teacher, but how you deal with it is more important than the failure itself.

Finally, in March 1988, we graduated from medical school, seven years after we had started. Not being unique to my narrative, the initial class size of fifty churned out only forty-five students at graduation. The attrition tells the story of how stressful it is to become a doctor.

Chapter 9

POSTGRADUATE EDUCATION

I did not like exposure to blood. That is why I fashioned my career around internal medicine and therapeutics. This is the field of medicine that allows me to heal people without cutting them open. It requires a detailed mastery of the various disease processes and tasks an astute intellectual ability. The experts make this second nature, which appears very easy to the uninitiated. We revered the British doctors with these clinical skills.

Soon after my internship in Ghana, I left the shores of Ghana for the United Kingdom to acquire these skills in internal medicine.

Medicine is a very delicate profession. Mistakes on the part of the clinician can lead to a devastating effect on the patient and even cause death. As a result, most developed countries require a doctor to be trained abroad to meet a certain standard before he or she is allowed to practice in that country. This is done through an examination process administered by the regulatory board of medicine. In the United Kingdom, the examination is acronymed PLAB, and in the United States, it is acronymed USMSLE.

The PLAB was designed to allow only the best foreign-trained doctors to practice in the United Kingdom. As a result, it must fail at least 30 percent of the candidates. It was also very expensive to register for this examination.

The foreign-trained doctor was required to pass this examination before being allowed to start the postgraduate training. With my limited funds, and perching with my sister Agnes in London, I prepared for this examination for three months and passed the first time. It was a very significant moment. For the first time, I could practice medicine in a foreign land and earn money.

Postgraduate training in England took about four years. It consisted of six months of rotation through the various departments of medicine in varied hospitals all over the United Kingdom. I started at Greenwich Hospital in London and then went to Wagan Royal Infirmary, Worcester Royal Infirmary, Nevill Hall Hospital in Abergavenny, and finally the University Hospitals in Cardiff, where I settled.

I worked for an additional three years in various hospitals around Cardiff until I became bored after discovering my true self. I was very comfortable working as a doctor, but my potential had not been met. I had a lot more to offer than working for someone and being paid a salary. I wanted to be in control of how much I wanted to work, when I wanted to work, and where I wanted to work.

A short vacation to the United States cut the ice. I visited a mate in New Jersey who was working as an emergency-room doctor, Dr. Alifoe. Through my exploratory interrogation, he revealed how much less he was working and how much more he was making. When I returned to England, I knew the United States should be my next destination. This also required various regulatory examinations called USMLE.

I took six months to prepare for this examination. After an easy success in these three-step examinations, I was faced with where to go for the second postgraduate training. Coming to Chicago was a matter of random selection. I did not have a clue as to what to expect. I interviewed in Cook County Hospital, and I was selected on the spot.

My second postgraduate training was for three years, from 1997 to 2000. It was a boring three-year training for me. I was not challenged intellectually. I had already trained in England. But I had to do it to be able to practice in the United States. After graduating, I entertained the idea of subspecializing in gastroenterology. But after a second consideration, I thought I had had too much of schooling and had to stop and work.

Everyone has an accent. It depends on which part of the world you find yourself.

A professor with a thick American accent gave my first lecture in Cook County Hospital. It was a lecture on hygiene. I made out that he was cracking jokes during the lectures, and most of the students were laughing. I did not understand a word of what he was saying or why they were laughing. A difficulty understanding someone or being understood is a real challenge for foreigners. In medicine, where communication is a vital component of decision-making, it can be frustrating to both the doctor and the patient.

People you meet at the postgraduate level are at the pinnacle of academia. They are the selected few drawn from far and wide. My mates were Chinese, Indian, Jewish, and other Africans. They are, characteristically, nice and down to earth. They are the last friends you will make in academia. This is a privileged opportunity that must not be taken for granted. These are the people who will shape the future, either being in high positions in government or directing scientific research. And these are what my last academic friends have become.

Finally, I graduated from Cook County Hospital. Now the educational journey of the boy from the small village in Ghana had finally come to an end. I was now a full-fledged doctor ready to hit the roads in the United States. Looking back on this journey has humbled me. I feel very lucky and thankful to my parents for giving me that initial thrust with their pinkies.

Chapter 10

THE EXODUS

MY FAMILY MIGRATION

Humans are blessed with the ability of sharing ideas that benefit one another. We take it for granted when we pick up the phone and speak to someone in the remotest part of the world or turn on the switch and the light comes on. These simple actions are benefits we have derived from multiple human inventions that have been shared over the years and perfected for the advancement of humankind. Humanity will continue to follow this path of selflessness to the benefit of itself.

Imagine living in a world where each person lives for him- or herself and in a bubble of a selfish community that is self-reliant and oblivious to alien ideas. This seemingly secluded community would naïvely take its equilibrium as the norm and be happy with all of its functions and progress.

Compare members of this utopian society to someone living in the United States or Great Britain who has never traveled outside of his or her respective country before and, likewise, someone who has lived exclusively in Ghana or its remotest environ. Having lived in these worlds, I have come across many such people. They tend to have different perceptions of the world around them. A lot of these people are happy with the status quo and resistant to change.

Having moved from Ghana to work in Great Britain as a well-established doctor, I felt everything was great. I had everything I needed. I had a house and a car. I could afford most things. I was comfortable. I did not have to leave. I was in my own bubble in England. But when I visited the United States, I realized that things were done differently, and I could use the livelihood there to improve myself.

In contrast to the one living in the utopian community, the ones who have traveled or at least been exposed to an external environ behave differently. They appear more complete and are more tolerant to other societal nuances. They are ready and willing to assimilate the pieces of their alien environments to enhance their own complexity. They are otherwise deemed seasoned.

"Travel and see" is the mantra we hear all the time. From the beginning of creation, mankind has moved from one location to another for all sorts of reasons. Some people are forced from their comfortable environments by natural disasters and wars. Others want a change of scenery or just want to explore. Whatever the reason for the movements of people from one environment to the other, it always impacts a change in the immigrant and the receiving community. This change is the result of using bits and pieces of your new environment, which has already been created by the ideas of its inhabitants.

By virtue of education, I moved out of my comfort zone in the village to have a medical education in the country's capital city of Accra. This gave me the opportunity to live in two worlds and be able to compare the styles of a village life and a city life.

Cleary, the villagers were living in a bubble. This was facilitated by the absence of television sets and the Internet, which would have enabled them to see the world around them. The villagers went about their normal farming duties, lived off the earth, and subsisted in a meager economy. Life was simple. They had only one another to compare themselves with.

On the other hand, the city was overflowing with many activities other than farming. My first impression of the city was that everything cost more than in the village. But I soon realized that you earned more money for a job done, and the resultant lifestyle was more elevated.

After much consideration, I decided I should move all my family from the village to live in the capital, Accra. It was during my first year as a doctor, and my personal status was not as strong. My sister Agnes, who lived in London, had just bought a home in Ghana and was happy for someone to live in the house. So I moved everyone into the three-bedroom house in Accra.

It was my job to feed them, clothe them, and settle them. I helped them in new business activities or education they wanted to undertake. It was financially and physically tasking in the first year. But being inherently enterprising too, most of them adapted very quickly and found their respective niches.

Today, the positive effect of this mass emigration of my family from the village to the city is even more apparent in their children and grandchildren. Their newfound home in the city allowed them to be even more advanced than their parents. They all had the secondary education that eluded many of their contemporaries in the village. Some went on to have tertiary education and vocational training in nursing, catering, and so on.

On occasions like Christmas and Easter, the second and third generations return to the village to celebrate. One can easily see the contrast between living in the two worlds, village and city.

Movement of people from one location to the other is a divine creation. The world was created for all humankind, but humankind has become selfishly territorial and put in boundaries. Nature's will for people's movement will continue until there is complete equilibrium.

One can enumerate many benefits that have been derived from such intermingling of peoples. Ghana, certainly, has largely benefited from the absence of tribal wars. The scale of tribal war that occurred in Ruanda can never be imagined in Ghana.

The first president of Ghana, in his wisdom, created a secondary and tertiary education to be merit based rather than community based. Therefore, a student can have this education anywhere in the country as long as he or she has the qualifying grades. This created an automatic mingling of all the tribes in the country. This early integration resulted in unconscious reconditioning of the mind that we are all the same people. Through friendship and intermarrying, a melting pot of tribes has been created in Ghana, allowing peace and harmony.

Often the newcomers in a society are conscious of creating better lives for themselves, and this leads to advancement of the community or humankind as a whole. We do not have to look too far to notice the impact of the contributions of newcomers like Einstein. Perhaps it is fair to say that newcomers in any society are more progressive than the indigents. This is debatable, but it is my opinion.

Chapter 11

PROFESSION

Medicine is a calling to me. Helping other people is my second nature. Taking the Hippocratic Oath was like preaching to the choir. Like most doctors, I practice to the best of my ability. After each encounter with a patient, I can go to sleep knowing that I have delivered my best. I practice not to make money, but money came to me because I gave my best. I am blessed with the power of attracting patients without solicitation. If I cannot satisfy a patient, the patient is usually the problem.

The experience I acquired from practicing medicine on three different continents gave me a good insight into the dynamics of medicine and how it affects a doctor's decision-making process and patient care. I am able to compare and contrast medicine practiced in a typical third-world country, a socialist British system, and the capitalist American system.

I practiced medicine for three years in Ghana, in a so-called third-world country setting, from 1988 to 1991. In this system, the patients are poor and cannot afford much. There was no health-care insurance policy. All the patients must pay cash for their services. There were government hospitals and many private counterparts and clinics.

A trained doctor is equipped with the knowledge of resources needed to make a clinical decision and advise the appropriate therapy. When faced with a complicated patient who had inadequate financial means, this task could be very daunting. We relied heavily on our clinical skills acquired to make the best judgment. Therapy was then dependent on this judgment. For simple disease processes, this was very easy. Difficult cases required more laboratory work, which could be costly.

Medicine is science, and when there is no laboratory data to back or dispute a hypothesis, we are unable to administer the right treatment. I have known patients who walked away from the realm of modern medicine to try herbal medicine because we failed to make the right diagnosis as the result of the financial limitation. Obviously, this was like going from a frying pan to fire, but what did they have to lose?

On the other hand, there were situations when we knew what to do for the patient, but either the patient could not afford the treatment, or the technology was not available in the hospital.

I had a patient who died from an acute asthma attack. This was a preventable death. Simple asthma is easy to treat. But when faced with this patient whose airways were completely closed, the only option left was to run a tube down the airways and put her on a breathing machine. The hospital did not have an intensive care unit, and this breathing machine was not available.

I saw many patients with kidney failure who needed dialysis. There were only two dialysis machines in my days in the whole country. You dared not have a kidney failure. Not only were there not enough machines to serve the population, but the patients who needed it most could not afford the cost of treatment. This is just an example of the many frustrations that well-meaning doctors have to deal with.

Surgery was a bit more rewarding than internal medicine. It was either repairing something or removing something, and the surgeons were very good at. However, postoperative complications could be very problematic, and the lack of an intensive care unit made this very scary.

I had a relative who was treated for a bowel obstruction. Everything went well, but he died the day of discharge from a blood clot in the lung. This was a preventable death.

Lack of education in the general population was a huge impediment in the outcome of patient care. I have seen patients come to the hospital with late stages of every disease process you can imagine. Who would think that simple diarrhea and vomiting can kill a child? Yes, they did, because of lack of education to seek prompt medical attention.

In the eyes of a doctor, it is very pathetic to see people die of preventable deaths. In the general population, though, there is a cultural dictum that God gives and God takes away. This dictum has created the inertia that exists in many communities to address the cause of death and institute mechanisms for prevention. It plays into the paradigm of life expectancy of fifty-five to sixty-five.

As pathetic as it may sound, we saved many lives with the limited resources available. After all, in medicine, 80 percent of the time we deal with common things, and the common diseases are easy to spot and treat. They do not need elaborate diagnostic workups. The patients are able to afford this treatment, and the herbalist and the juju man are kept at bay. If one looks at it this way, doctors are doing a good job.

The unfortunate 20 percent of patients had conditions that required more resources. Many of these patients died as martyrs. But their demise was not in vain. The energy they left behind has urged many doctors to agitate for advanced diagnostic and therapeutic facilities in Ghana.

Today, thirty years after I first practiced medicine in Ghana, the country can boast of the availability of services close to the first world. The limitation is cost, but at least it's available. There is also a health-care scheme, which is in its infancy. At least the country is on the right track.

Because of the lack of health education and cost, the country is not set up for preventive medicine. The point is, the earlier you catch a disease process, the easier and less costly it is to treat. This is a huge problem and contributes immensely to the abrogated life expectancy in Ghana. The older one is, the more likely there will be disease. Fortunately, a lot of these diseases, when detected early, can be treated or prevented. Life expectancy in the whole country can be prolonged if preventive medicine is instituted.

The culture of attributing disease and death to the force of witchcraft or bad spirits is frustrating to the medical practitioner in this part of the world. The phenomenon is more prevalent in the low socioeconomic group. It contributes to delays in seeking early medical intervention. Most times, patients would try to redress the so-called spirits by going to the herbalist or the juju man as their first port of call. When all failed, they would then present themselves to modern medicine, at which point it may be too late. I have seen paralysis from tuberculosis of the spine as a result of failed herbal treatment; this condition could easily be treated with six to nine months of antibiotics. Change of this mind-set requires a lot of public education orchestrated by the governmental public health institutions.

From 1991 to 1997, I practiced medicine in the United Kingdom. Coming from an African medical practice to a first-world medical system was a culture shock. One of my senior colleagues, who was familiar with my background, simply put it to me as, "Here you can order any test you want." This crudely summarized the abundance the health-care system presented to both the practitioner and the patient.

The United Kingdom has a single-payer system, the government. It is called the National Health System, NHS. There is also a private system called BUPA. This is an alternative for people with money or for anyone not happy with the NHS. The NHS provides free medical service for anyone in the country. All one needs to do is present oneself to any medical facility, and that person will receive very good medical care, and no one will ask for money.

The National Health System has a family practice setting, called general practice or GP, and the hospital setting. The GP system is run by family medicine doctors. Patients are assigned to a GP system based on their zip codes. There are no crossovers. When you move from one locality to another, you are assigned a GP in your new locality.

The hospital system is for admissions and specialist outpatient clinics. The doctors are grouped in a hierarchical system. The boss is called the consultant. The consultant has, in decreasing order of seniority, a registrar, senior house officer, and house officer. Each of these junior doctors is on a training path to become a consultant one day or branch into a GP system. The consultant is by specialty of medicine. Most hospitals have only one consultant per specialty. The consultant is the highest paid in the NHS system, and it is strictly by appointment by a local medical board. It is a very biased appointment system as it favors only the British-born citizens. For a foreign medical doctor with an accent like me, it was a remote possibility.

I practiced medicine in the hospital system. I rotated through all the departments of medicine during my training. I am more adept in pulmonary medicine because I spent more time in this field in Wales. This is the locality of Great Britain, where, because of coal mining, there existed the most complicated forms of lung disease. My boss, Dr. Gordon Thomas, was adjudged the unfriendliest person in the hospital. When I discovered why he was not liked, he became my closest friend. Dr. Thomas was very knowledgeable and practiced medicine to absolute perfection. His mouth beaters were the ones who were wishy-washy in their acts. I believed in good practice, and I picked my skills from Gordon.

The cost of medical care in a system like the NHS was very controlled. There was practically no wastage in the GP system. There was no duplication of testing. There was no doctor shopping for drug seekers. The doctors were paid for good work and rewarded based on quality measures they performed and outcomes.

The hospital system initially had a lot of waste and redundancy, but this was quickly controlled. I rose through the ranks of the hierarchy system in the hospital from a house officer to a registrar. The registrar was the bottleneck and the professional grave for the aspiring doctor. You could find yourself with this title for the rest of your life or until you got fed up and left. The system tried to mitigate this frustration by creating an ad hoc position called staff grade doctor, paid a bit more money than the registrar. This was a dead-end street for the aspiring doctor. Most registrars ended up taking these positions.

Patient satisfaction was generally good. They did not have to pay any bills, or their bill was paid up front from the high taxation system. The only disadvantage was a long waiting list for elective surgeries. But there was the private sector, BUPA, designed to take care of patients with no patience and who have cash to spare.

The medical health-care system in this nation is very good. This translates into a prolonged life expectancy of eighty-one years today. There is job satisfaction for the doctor, who has all the resources available at his or her disposal to perform his or her duty.

Being salaried by the government, doctors delivered care unbiased by any financial gains. There were no lawsuits for malpractice, and this greatly reduced the cost of care. They did not order a test just because they wanted to make extra money or just in case a lawyer asked why a test was not performed. Medicine was practiced in its purity in this system, and the doctors had a lot of resources to work with.

My typical workday started at about 9:00 a.m. and lasted until 3:00 p.m. Every fourth day, we stayed in the hospital for the twenty-four-hour call. During the weekend call, which was every fourth weekend, we stayed in the hospital from Saturday at 9:00 a.m. until work was over on Monday at 3:00 p.m. The hospital work was very exciting and rewarding. It was the first time I ever said to myself that dying is difficult. We could do a lot to sustain and prolong life.

The calls were draining on the doctors' health. It changed me from a deep sleeper to a light sleeper. Prior to being a doctor, I could sleep through a hurricane. During these calls, we were like life vigilantes on persistent high alert. From wherever you were, whether being in the bathroom or sleeping, you must be at the location of a cardiac arrest code within three minutes. You caught sleep whenever you could but were ready to jump out of your bed at any minute to attend to a code. It took me a long time to adjust to this mode of work. Now I am a very light sleeper, and I am benefiting from this drill with my ability to think, function, and make quick medial decisions with automaticity.

One time I was the registrar attending to a code of cardiac arrest. The patient, in his seventies, was a coal miner with a severe lung disease from coal dust and long-term smoking. He had been on supplemental oxygen for many years. He was on his last legs. During the morning rounds, I proudly presented to my boss, Dr. Thomas, how the team was able to bring the patient back from a cardiac arrest. Dr. Thomas was expressionless, seemingly unimpressed.

During the tea break, he politely said that I should have let this guy go. Part of our job was to relieve suffering. The patient died a few weeks later. Discerning between sympathy and empathy is very important, and it is a skill you acquire on the job. A doctor has to learn when to say that enough is enough for a patient.

I enjoyed working as a doctor in the United Kingdom. The pay was good, but it was depressing when deductions on your pay slip amounted to over 40 percent for up-front payment of all the benefits that living in a quasi-socialist society entitles you to. Some of these entitlements include free health care. I could have resigned myself to living in this system forever, but my constitution was not made for stagnation. There was more that I could offer this world. I wanted the independence to control how much work I could do and not settle for a salaried job.

The calling came eventually when one of my Indian colleagues, who was then a stagnated senior registrar, was asked to cover for a consultant who was on vacation. Clearly this colleague qualified as a consultant. His only disqualifications were that he was Indian, had an accent, and was not born in Britain. Aware of my own disqualifications, not unlike my colleague's, I did not want to be counted among the lot of stagnated registrars. At that point, I felt that America would offer me more choices as a doctor. Within a few months, I prepared for the three-step USMLE examinations that enabled me to gain a postgraduate position in the Windy City of Chicago.

Practicing medicine in the United States is a real challenge for a doctor cultured in Great Britain. My initial disappointment was when I witnessed a patient presenting with severe shortness of breath coming to a private hospital. The front desk staff would not allow the patient through to be seen until the patient presented her insurance information. It makes sense there, but I found it very strange. The British system would normally not bring up the subject of money when treating a patient. Even though everyone wants to be paid for a job done, the system was not structured to center around money.

Television advertisements of medical products also got me. It is uncommon to see doctors advertising themselves for their services. For the newcomer, it sounds strange to see a television advertisement for medical products like medications, hospital services, or clinics.

My British in-laws felt very uncomfortable when they visited us in Chicago one day. My daughter was about ten years old. We were watching television together when a commercial for Viagra started to run. The looks on their faces spelled out their embarrassment to be watching this advertisement with their granddaughter. They quickly turned off the television to avoid my daughter listening to the commercial.

Another shocker to the new foreign doctor was the big deal about medical malpractice. It was very strange to see a television commercial advertising that patients with medical mishaps should call such-and-such law firm to sue their doctors. British-cultured doctors go the extra mile to present to their patients the best possible care. Both patient and doctor know that a bad outcome could result from the delivery of medical care. Hence, it sounds strange for a patient to sue his or her own doctor, who has delivered his or her best.

One more strange thing I noticed was that the patients were free to see any doctor they wanted, irrespective of where they lived. Immediately I could smell unnecessary duplication of services.

These short scenarios recapitulate the medical system I was suddenly faced with. It is not hard to figure out that this setup would drive the cost of medical delivery through the roof. The high cost of medical delivery in the United States does not translate into longevity, with an average life expectancy that stands at 79.3 years. This is, ironically, much lower than socialist-medicine Britain.

The American medical system has very few government hospitals and myriads of private clinics and hospitals. Each of these medical facilities offers the best possible care in order to attract patients in this competitive system.

There is the Medicare insurance system for the old, Medicaid for the poor, and private insurance for workers. But there are many more people in between who are not covered by any insurance.

Soon after my second postgraduate training, I was first employed by a mobile doctor company. I was given a car, and my job was to drive to the patient's house to deliver health care. These patients were usually old and not able to leave their homes to see a doctor. I enjoyed doing it, but after a year, I decided to work for myself.

For me, it was a very easy process, and within six months, I had a full-fledged medical clinic based in Michael Reese Hospital in Chicago. I started dreaming big that I wanted to own a hospital. But to get there, I needed to test the ground first. My keen interest got me closer to the hospital chief executive officer, Dr. E. Beckman. I helped reduce the waste in their admission process. This saved the hospital, which was going through a great deal of financial problems, a lot of money.

Soon I was invited to be a member of the board of directors of the hospital. I was honored and felt very privileged and thankful to Dr. Beckman for the position. This board was faced with the possibility of the hospital's closure and was tasked to prevent this from happening. Serving for about three years on the board equipped me with a great deal of business foresight that I call on in my own ventures.

To continue my journey of owning my own hospital, I built a mini hospital first. I called it Korle-Bu Medical Center. I acquired a piece of land on the South Side of Chicago and built a three-level medical center. I called this a hospital without a bed. It had an ambulatory clinic, a dental clinic, an eye clinic, cardiac diagnostic, physical therapy, and many other services. When it opened in 2006, it was my wow moment. Everything was going well until the American financial crisis in 2008.

When the bubble finally burst in the year 2008, the company, on the advice of an astute Chicago lawyer, went under the protection of Chapter 7. This American law of insolvency allowed me to restructure the company, which was behind on its debt commitments. With a slimmed-down operation, I emerged from Chapter 7 with a newly formed company, Dr. John Awah & Associates, Ltd. Many jobs were saved as a result.

When you re-walk a path where a snake previously bit you, you could find yourself bitten again by the same snake because you did not learn. I restructured Dr. John Awah & Associates with a new team of good workers and removed services that were not profitable. I gave ownership of my own building to the bank and became a tenant. I continued to work the same number of hours I had previously. Within a few months, I saw a huge turnaround in the bottom line. However, at this point of comfort, I foresaw that it would be short-lived if things remained status quo. The future of health care in the United States was about to change, and I was right. I entertained the thought that it was time to do something different. Other business interests started rippling through my skull. When this crystallized, I sold the now profitable medical practice to Metro-South Hospital in Chicago for a good sum of money. (I will elaborate on the investment in the chapter on business ventures.) The hospital decided that it was interested only in buying my services and not my name. They were right, and I was happy.

I became a salaried employee of Metro-South Hospital in Chicago. Eighteen months into my two-year contract, I became unchallenged by being an employee rather than an employer. I gave my one-month notice and resigned.

I started a new medical practice in Chicago, this time for selected patients who were housebound. I learned from my previous experience of ambulatory practice that certain must-have overheads significantly eat into the profit margin. I then fashioned my new practice to take away almost all the overhead, like rent, a receptionist, medical assistants, utilities, and the like.

Since we are now in the cyber world, you could have a mobile office that you could take to patients' homes. Everything can be accessed from the cloud. Homebound patients need a doctor to attend to them. That reduces the costly hospital admissions if they are attended to promptly in the comfort of their homes. They can call me anytime, and I do not need an appointment to see them as long as I give them a two- to four-hour prior warning of my visit. This model suits all my patients and me.

This is the nature of my current medical practice. My office is located in a small corner of my house, equipped with a laptop computer and a three-in-one fax, copy, and printer. My wife is the manager, doubling up as a mother to my three-year-old daughter, Ama. I have two physician assistants and a podiatrist. I have a remote part-time biller. The practice is now devoid of the traditional medical office overhead, and I cannot think of anything more I can do to better the bottom line.

The dynamics of patient care in the United States are shaped by many factors, including the culture of freedom of choice on behalf of the patient, patient exposure to new technology and medicines, cutting-edge medicine being practiced, the ability to consume new medicines irrespective of cost, and the lobbying power of pharmaceutical companies. The most precious commodity being life, coupled with these factors, has made it possible for the health-care business to thrive even in bad economic times.

There is hardly any waiting time for any procedure, and the patient is spoiled for choice. There is abundant employment for highly trained medical staff members, and they make very good livings out of it. The downside of this abundance and easy accessibility of medical services in the United States is the high cost of health-care delivery, which does not translate into a correspondent longevity compared to Great Britain. Ghana will make progress, but it must fight this from different fronts, including improving health literacy and dispelling the superstitions associated with diseases.

Chapter 12

THE THREE MOST INTRIGUING PATIENTS

In this chapter, I will recount the story of selected patients I personally treated from the three continents where I practiced medicine. I am hoping their cases will help enlighten the reader on the health-care practices in the three worlds and generate a discussion on the cultural differences with respect to health care. While I am not able to use real names for these patients even if I remembered them, I am using pseudo-names in order to personalize the cases. The cases are by no means meant to undermine the health-care practice in each country but to throw a light on true occurrences that I personally encountered. I would reserve all comments on each case to the reader who will have different opinions depending on their origin and background.

GHANA:

I was a fresh graduate from the medical school, and my first posting was in obstetrics and gynecology. This was not a field I was particularly interested in since I did not like exposure to blood. However, it was a prerequisite for our training, and I had to do it. Moreover, unlike the morning reports in internal medicine, which were wrapped around difficult cases with no real tangible solutions, obstetrics often resulted in a happy ending of real crying babies. So the going was good.

One day, around lunchtime in the outpatient, we were presented with Adjoa, who was in her early twenties in labor. This case was assigned to me to manage as an intern. Examination of Adjoa revealed there was a cord prolapse. This was an obstetrics emergency, meaning that the cord was coming before the baby. If labor was allowed to proceed naturally, there would be a cutoff of blood supply to the baby, and the baby would almost certainly not survive.

With this in mind, my consultant quickly arranged with the operating theater for an emergency cesarean section.

Transporting the patient from the outpatient clinic to the operating theater required an ambulance transport. When everything was ready for the patient to be transported, the ambulance driver could not be found. Being a very religious Muslim, he was found praying nearby but could not be disturbed until the prayer was over.

Since this was an emergency, the most obvious thing to do was drive the ambulance myself. Luckily I found the keys in the ambulance, and with no time to spare, I drove the patient to the operating theater.

The surgery was successful. A bouncy baby boy was born, nameless because by tradition, babies are not given names until they are one week old.

However, with the scanty prenatal care Adjoa received during her pregnancy, she had gone into labor with a very low blood count. The little blood loss during surgery compounded this into severe anemia. She was pale, and the heart was ticking away very fast in response to the low blood count. The only treatment was a blood transfusion.

As usual, Adjoa's blood was drawn, typed, and cross-matched. In the postnatal ward, while Adjoa was resting and ready to become a new mother, she received the blood that was meant to save her life.

About one hour into the blood transfusion, Adjoa became unresponsive and died. She had had a severe reaction to the blood she received.

This was investigated thoroughly by the hospital when they found out that even though the labeling on the blood bag matched Adjoa's credentials, the content was a severe deviation from her blood type. This was a laboratory error. I cannot remember what the consequence was for the technician, but at the time, it would not have been far from a mere reprimand.

For the family of the deceased, there was obvious crying and acrimony, but they would be pacified by well-wishers that God gave and God had taken away.

For me it was an eye-opener into the medical world of the mishaps that can happen beyond one's control. It was a sad end of a case I had put all my heart in to manage.

UNITED KINGDOM:

Unlike many doctors trained in the underdeveloped countries, those trained in advanced countries may never have seen and treated certain types of infectious diseases. My medical training in Ghana allowed me exposure to a significant cross section of many infectious diseases that are very rare in developed countries like Britain.

During my journey in Britain as a postgraduate doctor, I rotated through Nevill Hall Hospital in Abergavenny, Wales. I was the only doctor of color in this hospital. I was second in command on the pulmonary medicine team headed by my boss, Dr. Gordon Thomas. There were three other teams, and together we took turns in admitting new patients.

One day, on my team's off day, I was in the little town, shopping, when surprisingly, I had a page from my boss. Since there was no luxury of mobile phones at the time, I located a pay-phone booth in the mall to return the call.

On the phone, my boss asked me if I had seen and managed a case of tetanus before. I said yes and asked why. Then he explained that the on-call team had a case of tetanus and that none of them had ever seen or managed this condition. Since he had a Ghanaian trained doctor on his team they wanted us to take over the management. I said I was happy to do that.

It was a good decision by the admitting team and for the patient since no patient would want to be treated by a doctor with no experience, especially for such a life-threatening condition.

I quickly returned to the hospital. I saw an elderly Caucasian, Mrs. Smith, who a few days prior had been working in her garden when a wood splinter got into her little finger. This had been removed, but it left behind an area of painful redness. She presented to the hospital when her jaws were locking and she had increasing difficulty swallowing.

Since I had seen and managed such a case before at the fever unit in Ghana, I confirmed the diagnosis, and the boy from the African village took charge.

I became my boss's boss, not because I was an expert in infectious disease but because I was more experienced in managing this condition.

But as the saying goes, it is never over until it is over, and anything could go wrong. It was a life-threatening condition, and I was solely responsible for the outcome. Moreover, in this part of the world where there was hardly any exposure to colored persons, especially one who would save your life, it was not uncommon to hear an inner voice saying I had to prove myself before I would be trusted. The silver lining here was that, unlike Ghana, we had all the backups and supports needed to sustain life, and the chances of recovery were much higher.

We transferred Mrs. Smith to the intensive care unit, and with the help of machines, we supported her life throughout the initial serious phase of the condition, assisting her with breathing and feeding. We managed the germs and the toxins with medications that were readily available.

During this time, I consulted with the patient's family but did not try to raise false hopes. I calmed their nerves and made them feel comfortable to accept the outcome of this serious condition.

Many days of turbulence followed, which involved consulting those with other specialties of medicine for their input. Finally, the day dawned on Mrs. Smith's life when all the vital signs began to line up in the right direction. Gradually we began to back off on the strong medications and allowed the patient to gain consciousness.

One observation in medicine is that when a patient initially gains consciousness from a coma, they feel exhausted, aloof, and indifferent while the family is in extreme elation, and rightly so; the patient is completely oblivious to the whole event, and time is the factor that brings them to realization.

At the bedside of Mrs. Smith, when she finally came around, I could feel the relief and joy of her family when they hugged me with big smiles. With the help of my team and the backup of the hospital, I had provided leadership that extended the life of Mrs. Smith.

USA:

The worse nightmare for a physician in the United States is to be sued for a medical mishap. Not uncommonly in this country, there are advertisements in public places and on national television from law firms soliciting business from patients and family members who think they have suffered consequences from medical malpractice. Some of these advertisements seek not to accept any money until the case is won.

The first time I was exposed to this, I was taken aback that the patient you are currently treating with your whole heart and in good faith could one day turn against you and take you to court should anything go wrong. Usually it does not happen, but when it does, it could be very daunting.

Against this backdrop, I managed Mr. Jackson, who was in his sixties. He was a heavy alcoholic. One winter day, he was very drunk, and while on his way home, he fell on a sheet of ice and sustained a neck injury. The ambulance took him to the nearest hospital, where he was diagnosed with quadriplegia, meaning total paralysis of all his limbs.

A permanent hole was drilled into his windpipe, called a tracheostomy, to aid his breathing and another one in his stomach, called a gastrostomy tube, to aid his feeding. A strict regime of care was instituted, which included scheduled feeding and toileting of the tracheostomy.

He was moved to a nursing home as his permanent residence because his family could not take care of this strict regimen. For the next four years until he became my patient, Mr. Jackson developed many complications, including multiple bedsores. To make matters worse, his wife was a difficult personality, and her expectations were very tasking to the nursing staff. This generated a discord with each nursing home he went to. And anytime Mr. Jackson was admitted to a hospital, it was an opportunity to get rid of him. As a result, he was shifted from one nursing home to another.

It was in the course of this nursing-home hopping that Mr. Jackson became my patient. He was randomly assigned to me by the nursing home administration.

Seeing Mr. Jackson for the first time, I felt very sorry for him. He was contracted, had bedsores on his back, had a tube in his neck requiring suctioning every half hour, had a feeding tube, and had a call bell like a whistle attached to his head.

I managed Mr. Jackson for the next year and a half in two nursing homes. I created a rapport with his very demanding wife and yielded to all her demands, which most of the time were associated with creating more tasks for the nursing staff.

Then, one night Mr. Jackson passed away in his sleep, as if to say he had had enough. I called his wife and consoled her and offered my sincere condolences. I told her to contact me if there was anything I could do to help. I thought the case was closed.

About four years later, I received a call from his last nursing home saying an attorney wanted to talk to me about Mr. Jackson. Initially I could not recall who Mr. Jackson was nor the case, until the attorney refreshed my memory. Then he told me the family was suing the nursing home, the hospital that first treated his broken neck, the ambulance that took him to the hospital when he fell, and all medical staff involved in his care.

It was a huge case to describe, but the long and short of it was that the family responded to a TV advertisement from law firms for suits against wrongful deaths in nursing homes. The net was cast as wide as possible to drag as many people into it in an attempt to find fault. At the onset, the nursing home where he had died offered to settle for a quarter million dollars. This was cheaper than to allow the case to drag into a protracted legal course. The family rejected the offer.

In an attempt to get more money, they had to find fault with the most insured in the net. Since I was the most insured, to the tune of $1 million per case, I became the obvious target. And this was how I got dragged into the case.

I was assigned a brilliant young lawyer from my insurance company. She invited me to her office to go over the motive of the case and prepare me for my defense. It turned out that the suing party was not happy with my most probable cause of death on the death certificate. Considering all the comorbidities that Mr. Jackson had and the detailed care he received in the nursing home, I suggested a heart problem as the most probable cause of death for him dying in his sleep.

A deposition was set up before the main court trial to see if they could find fault with my care. If they succeeded, then they would present me to the judge and punch holes in the medical care I had given Mr. Jackson. A sympathizing jury could then be on their side and result in a big booty.

The deposition was set up in a huge conference room in downtown Chicago. There were four attorneys from the suing party against my attorney and me.

The whole scene was captured on a video recorder and also by a court clerk typing away every word I spoke. The most striking thing I remember of it today is the clerk complaining about my accent and saying that I was speaking too fast.

The deposition lasted for about four hours, with a half-hour break. It was designed to make the probable cause of death a lung infection, which they would link to poor care of the patient's tracheotomy tube. Then both I and the nursing home would be sued together.

It was a very tense moment, and the air throughout the four hours was still. All their four lawyers specializing in various aspects of medical malpractice questioned me. The key was not to contradict myself. This was the game they played with me over and over again. My astute lawyer directed the proceedings and pointed out unfair questions and raised multiple objections. It was a great relief when it was all over.

However, the worst part of it all was the waiting for about four weeks as they reviewed the tapes and the transcript to see if they had enough evidence leaning their way to convince a jury of malpractice.

One afternoon, my attorney called. As soon as I saw her number, my heart began to thump. Then she said she had the verdict. And without wasting much time, she told me I had been exonerated. Moreover, the charges had all been dropped by the other party, and they were going to close the case.

The relief was indescribable. It was this case that engrained in me the need for documentation in my medical practice. If it is not written, it never happened!

Chapter 13

BUSINESS ADVENTURES

Successful people are all endowed with certain characteristics. I believe that these characteristics are partly genetic and partly environmental. The genetic component is a gift from the Creator that allows them to think outside the box and take risks without fear. They are not perturbed by failure. They are blessed with so much inherent motivation that when they fall, they pick up the pieces, brush off the dust from their behinds, and move on. These people are leaders and not followers. In fact, they make bad employees. They are always looking for deficiencies in the environment to take advantage of. In addition to all this, there may also be a personal triggering factor, which could be a mishap, that sparks the whole machinery of their business-mindedness.

This theory, which I self-generated, applies very well to most successful businesspeople. Test this against the hosts of the popular American reality show *Shark Tank*.

No schooling can teach you how to be entrepreneurial, and at the tender age of fifteen, I started thinking of my business journey alongside my schooling. When I discovered myself, I had all the ingredients already present. This was sparked by the financial stress I put on my parents when they offered to give me that needed secondary education, the most vital and rare determining step, as found in a chemical reaction.

During the second year, when I was offered the government scholarship to pursue the free education, I told my parents that the scholarship would start during the second trimester. I collected the school fees they had given me for the first trimester and invested it in my first business equipment.

I bought myself a twelve-exposure black-and-white camera. It was the type that looked like a small metal box and had a viewfinder located on the upper end. It was a very rudimentary camera compared to present-day cameras. It was all manually operated. The skill was in the ability to manually adjust the speed and the aperture by reading the weather. The twelve images were captured on film, which was developed in a darkroom into negatives. Then, with a light source shining through the negatives, the images were captured onto photographic paper, which was then washed in cold water, dried, and packaged.

I wanted to ease the financial burden of my parents, who were by this time about to send my younger brother Steve to a secondary school. The time was ripe for me to start my first business at age sixteen. I counted the days to my next vacation. I was going to be the only photographer resident in the village. I found the niche in the environment and the sparkle from circumstances beyond my control.

My first vacation after the acquisition of my equipment came eventually. At age sixteen, I was poised to start making money. I did not have any working capital, so I borrowed money from my sister Mamle. This was used to purchase twelve-exposure black-and-white film. By word of mouth, I advertised my new business. Suddenly I hit gold. There was a baptism in the Roman Catholic church. I was invited to be the photographer for the occasion. I quickly calculated how much money I was going to make in my head. I was very excited but very nervous. I was not trained to use this camera. I just read a bit of the instructions that came along with it, but I was confident I would get it right.

The baptism was over. I took about three rolls of film. I was ready to make my first profit. I was at the photographic shop the next day in the nearest big city to develop the film and print the photographs. How they would come out was all I was thinking of.

When the owner asked if I had been trained to use the camera, my heart sank, and my legs turned to jelly. Some of the pictures were without heads, others were very black, many more were blurred, and in a handful I could just about make out their faces. In fact, none of the pictures came out as expected.

That was my first failure in business. I dreaded to break the news to my clients, and I broke the promise to pay back my sister for the money she had lent me. I went into hiding for many days in the village to avoid my clients, who were anxious to see their memorable photographs. Eventually, when I came to terms with myself, I was able to face them and offer the explanation that it had been my first time. My sister forgave me.

With hesitation, I borrowed more money from my sister. This time I used the money to buy practice film and went to the photographic shop for training. My first mistake made me a quick learner. I perfected the trade very quickly, and by the end of the vacation, I was a confident photographer.

I used the profit to supplement my parents' money and got not only Steven but also the one following him, Narh, through a secondary education. I gave up the photographic business after I got into my sixth-form education to concentrate on my studies.

As a young businessman in my teens, I had more of an appetite for bigger things in the village and found another niche in the market: entertainment. I thought if I brought a popular live band to play in the village, I could make money off it. I approached a well-known band in the nearest city, Koforidua, called Okukuseku. They told me their fees. After quickly making a rough calculation in my head, I thought it would be profitable. I now had some money, so I paid the deposit and got a date for the show in the village. I then rented the venue in the village and paid the deposit. Then the band gave me a lot of posters, which I plastered in public places in the villages around. As there was no electricity and streetlights, the day was carefully chosen to fall on a full moon.

On the day of the show, you could feel the nerves of the village. With the full moon, you could see everyone out in the street waiting for the band to arrive. It was the first time the villagers would ever come close to a very popular music idol.

Then the time for the band to arrive came, and there was no sign of them. There were no telephones, so I could not make any calls. I started panicking. As the night advanced and still the band had not arrived, people started looking for me. I was still confident they would arrive, so I continued to boost their morale so they did not return to their villages. I gave up well past midnight when there was no sign of the band. I may have been about seventeen years old at the time, and I was not able to handle how disappointed I was. I was very ashamed.

The band did not give me my deposit, and I lost all my initial investment. But it was a lesson, and that was the last time I became a music promoter.

During my second year in medical school, our universities were closed because of student uprisings against the military government led by Jerry John Rawlings. The military government had instituted a policy that Ghana should be self-reliant and not dependent on other countries. The government banned the importation of essential commodities. There was scarcity of everything you can think of. All the shops were empty. To make matters worse, there was severe drought in Ghana that year. The farmers, relying on the rain for their crops, could not produce enough. There was a lot of hunger. I remember that in my village, people were eating tree roots to survive. One egg in a stew was the source of protein for a whole family, and it was that bad. My family had nothing, and I had to help.

I wanted to retail sugar, cooking oil, and rice. To get these products, I needed to smuggle them from the neighboring country, Togo. I set up a date and collected some money from my sister Mamle and my mother. It was their last bit of money, but I wanted to turn it around and give them back the capital and some dividends from my sales.

I teamed up with a uniformed policeman in the village who was also known to be in the smuggling business. We set off to Togo, which was a francophone country. The little French I had learned in school was a great advantage in my transaction. Unlike Ghana, Togo at the time had a stable government. Their shops were overflowing with the essential commodities missing in Ghana.

With our merchandise, we found a vehicle belonging to people who were adept at the smuggling business. They used unorthodox routes to get back to a main city interchange in Ghana. We set off in the night. The driver collected a bit of money from everyone on board to bribe those at the known checkpoints manned by corrupt Ghanaian soldiers. The journey was going well until about the third checkpoint. It may have been just past midnight.

With their powerful torch lights flashing in our faces and amid brandishing of their AK-47s, the soldiers ordered us to come out of the vehicle. We were all asked to identify our merchandise and ourselves. When it got to my turn, at which point my legs were almost like jelly, my uniformed police officer introduced me as his friend. When this was over, they ordered the only lady among us to stay behind with her goods. Then they ordered the driver to drive away. I looked behind when we were driving away, and it was pitch-black. While recovering from the shock, I was thinking about what would happen to the lady we had left in the hands of the very unfriendly soldiers.

We went through many more checkpoints, and the ordeal was routine: bribe our way through until we came to the very last checkpoint before the interchange city, Somanya. Here again we were faced with very unfriendly soldiers brandishing their AK-47s. It was daybreak, and the air was fresh and chilly. Amid their obvious facial expressions of victory at apprehending smugglers, they ordered everyone to again get off the vehicles and the driver to bring down all the merchandise. Then, one by one, they interrogated us. They came to know that I was one of the students calling on the military government to hand over power. This time my uniformed police friend could not protect me.

I was ordered at gunpoint to lie on the road. Then they ordered me to recite this sentence in the local language: "If I had known, I would not have been a smuggler." While I was reciting this sentence, they asked me to roll several times on the hard coal-tarred road. This went on for several minutes. I was too afraid to cry. And if I wanted to cry, I could not because crying would have been a defeat to my ego.

When they were all satisfied with the humiliation they meted out to me, they ordered me to get up. Then they asked me to go and tell all the other students to stop the talk, the agitation, and the rebellion against the military government. They confiscated all my merchandise, and I returned home empty-handed. My uniformed police friend was able to bring his smuggled goods home safely.

I never believed in ghosts until I was faced with a shadow and a smell that appeared to be one. This was during my timber-logging business in my third year of medical school. As I touched and let go of any business I could lay my hands on to see which one would stick, I had the rare opportunity of owning a chainsaw. I once visited a friend, David Padi, who worked for a power company, Valco, as a technician. As part of their Christmas bonus, he was given a chainsaw. David showed me this machine during my visit and asked me what I thought he should do with it. I said to him that he should give it to me for a few days.

I reached out to my uncle in the village to inquire about the business of renting out a chainsaw for the burgeoning logging business. When the answer was promising, I reached out to David and said I would put the machine to work and pay him back the market price for it. He was obliging and gave me the machine. Then I hired a chainsaw operator and took him to the village to start the logging business. We rented out the machine to the loggers; the operator would charge and collect the money. I would come to the village on weekends after school for the accounting. Soon we realized that the machine was too small for the tasks; it kept overheating and breaking down. The repairing cost quickly overtook the profit, and the business was not going well. I was falling behind with the repayment terms to my friend David.

Then, to add more insult, the machine operator fell ill. He developed a dental abscess that needed immediate attention. The nearest dentist was in the regional capital, Koforidua, about forty miles away. That needed two segments of transportation. One segment was fourteen miles, and the next was twenty-six, after a change to another vehicle. It was Saturday, and the outward journey was smooth. The operator was treated, and he felt a bit of relief. Now we had to find our way back to the village. It was getting dark, and by the time we made the first segment back, it was pitch-black. The last vehicle had left. We had fourteen miles to travel, and there was no vehicle. Imagine being stranded in a small village with no electricity and no hotel. That was exactly how it felt. The only option left for the two of us was to walk the fourteen miles in total darkness to our destination.

When faced with no choice, you just get on with the only one available. So it was, and we started walking. The air was fresh, and light winds were gently swinging the tree branches back and forth. It was pitch-black, but we could make out the direction of the road. The complete silence of the forest was frequently interrupted by the sounds of its inhabitants. The chorus of frogs and crickets was unmistakable. Then, in the distance were the yells of wild animals. Mosquitoes occasionally flew by our ears to take advantage and suck some blood.

Then the operator held my hand, pointed into the darkness ahead of us, and asked, "Did you see it?" I asked what, and he said, "The ghost." He asked me to look carefully and said I would see the shadow of a human being. I looked hard. I saw something. It was a dark human shadow. As we walked toward it in frigid fear, it became like a mirage and disappeared. At this time, I could hear my heart thumping very hard. Then the operator stopped me again and said, "Did you smell it?" I could smell the sweet aroma generating from the forest. That was a ghost smell, he explained. He was genuinely not making it up to scare me, but he thought I was a naïve city boy in the village, and he was used to these ghosts. If these were ghosts, I saw a multitude of them that night, and the encounter was not very pleasant.

After this nightlong ordeal, which would have been better if it were a nightmare, we finally arrived at our destination at about daybreak. We had walked the fourteen miles through a living hell, exhausted. The logging business folded not long after this, and I was back where I had started.

Then I lost my dad in the fourth year of medical school. This time it was a blessing in disguise. The trauma of losing a parent in the middle of career training is not fair. I wanted to show my appreciation to my dad after completing my training by doing something for him that would change his life. But to do this, I needed to complete my training first. And this had become the elephant in the room. My last source of funding, however small, dried out completely.

I had just had the opportunity, through Mr. Kapoor, to go to England to do an externship in medicine. When I was leaving, a guy from the medical store, Mr. Okine, gave me a kit and some money. He asked me to buy the same kit for him on my return. It was a pregnancy test kit, which he said was hard to come by in Ghana. So I did find the kit in London, and from a quick mental calculation I made, I figured out a very large profit margin. After working almost day and night in a McDonald's in London as a beef burger maker, I invested almost all the money I had made into pregnancy test kits. On my return, I immediately sold them through Mr. Okine, and I pocketed over 100 percent profit. This was the birth of my first-ever business incorporated in Ghana, called Laboratory and Clinical Supplies Ltd. It was in my final year of medical school, and I opened a shop in Akoto Lante, not too far away from the medical school. I had two initial employees, one to stay in the office and the other to go around and do marketing.

This business had no competition. It was the first medical supplies company in Ghana. It blossomed very quickly, and by the time I had my last lecture in medical school, I bought my first car, a BMW 7 Series. The most annoying part of this quick prosperity was that people thought the car belonged to my dad.

I quickly asked the supplier in London if I could become their sole agent in Ghana. From the records of the sales, they had no hesitation in agreeing to my request. Within a few months, we were presented with a letter from USAID in Ghana requesting a pro forma invoice for the supply of HIV kits for the Ministry of Health.

This was the takeoff time for my new company. Earlier, the USAID had approached the supplier in London for the pro forma invoice, but per our agreement, they were referred to their local agent, which was my company, Laboratory and Clinical Supplies Ltd. Our sales jumped from under $30,000 a year to over half a million.

I chalked up my first success after so many tries. I invested in lands and quickly built my first house in Accra for my mother. This was the point of no return for this village boy. I ran this business for many years until other people got wind that a medical supplies shop was lucrative. At this point, I had made enough money, and I was starting my second postgraduate training in Chicago. I transferred the remnants of the business to my younger brother Teye, and he was very happy.

The kerfuffle of the American economy in the late 1980s coupled with doing too many things at the same time sent Korle Medical Group into insolvency. The emergence of Dr. John Awah and Associates, Limited, a slimmed-down company in a better economy, produced a good result. But doing the same thing and making the same good money did not thrill me. I conceived the idea of early retirement from medicine and going into the business world. The only source of working capital was to sell Dr. John Awah and Associates, Limited.

Many choices of business came to mind, but the one that attracted me most was the gold mining business in Ghana. Contracts were awarded to backfill the huge hole in the ground created by the gold mining companies. Prospective contractors must possess a bulldozer, a series of excavators and dump trucks, and technical know-how. An acquaintance approached me to consider this business. After visiting the mining site, I discovered that this business was there to stay as long as the gold mining business continued. The numbers also looked good on paper. Theoretically, this was going to be a great retiring gig for me, and I could reinvest the proceeds.

The acquaintance, Edwin, was already in the business of renting out the heavy-duty machinery to the mining company and had the technical know-how. He and I decided to put our money together to acquire the needed equipment. I trusted him.

With that price tag of working capital in mind, I decided to sell my medical practice. The market was good, and I had two offers, one from the Advocate Group and the other from Metro-South Hospital, both in Chicago. Metro-South Hospital offered me a better deal, so I sold to them and signed a two-year contract to work for them. These were supposed to be my final years of medical practice and time to allow the mining business in Ghana to settle and start making some money.

The first six months of the mining business were quasi smooth. I saw regular accounting and very little dividend, which I felt was reasonable for a new business. However, the communications soon became few and far between, with the excuse of a bad telephone network in the field. Edwin's wife also got into the business and started controlling its affairs. The little dividends that were initially flowing to me then stopped for over six months. Alarm bells sounded in my mind, and when I visited Ghana again, the reception was no longer cordial. Without my knowledge, Edwin had used the equipment as collateral for a bank loan and started a new stone quarry business. This really infuriated me, and I called my lawyer on board. After dragging it on for a long time, we ended up in a commercial court in Accra.

During the trial, neither Edwin nor his lawyer showed up in court. The judge, after going through the trial of the case in the absence of Edwin, ruled in my favor. The court served Edwin a notice to pay me back my investment with interest.

The case has stalled there. Looking for Edwin, his property to liquidate, or his account to freeze is like looking for a needle in a haystack. At the time of writing this memoir, the case is still open.

My reinvented smart house-call practice in Chicago, which continues to grow, allowed me to continue my business ventures with little impact from the loss of the mining dream.

What do a doctor and a fish farm have in common? The answer is nothing. This was the challenge that became more intriguing for me to look at this business. I researched the statistics of world food production and saw a straggling net import of fish into Ghana, which has all the resources to be self-sufficient. There was obvious lack of education on scientific fish farming among Ghanaians. But the reality is that commercial farming is capital intensive, and government loans and grants are almost nonexistent in Ghana.

Since I had zero knowledge of raising fish, I felt that a taste of the fish farm business would be a very risky investment but, if successful, would be a good story. I recruited my elder sister Agatha, who had retired from the Ghana Armed Forces many years before. Together we did a preliminary inquiry with the Ministry of Fisheries in Ghana. They had very limited resources to offer a novice who wanted to invest in fish farming. They directed us to other farmers already in the business, who advised us with clenched hands.

With the meager advice from the existing farmers and the reassurance that it was an extremely good business, we acquired a piece of land on the bank of Volta Lake. Agatha relocated to this village, Kpeve, and, amid the fauna and wild snakes, set up a camp in the middle of the forest on the piece of land.

We got a cage in the river and bought a set of ten thousand fingerlings. Unlike the other farmers, who had started with multiple cages, we had only one. The idea was to feed these fingerlings until they reached the size of consumption at about five to six months. The concept was no different from a business plan that reads like a well-oiled machine. I have seen many businesses that have failed in my life by this time, and I did not hold my breath for what sounded too good to be true.

After six months of waiting to make our first profit in the fish business, we were faced with a huge loss. We harvested four thousand instead of the supposed ten thousand fish. In business, people tend to tell you the sweet side of the story. Novices fall for this, to their detriment. I did not fall for this. The one cage we had started with was to test the hypothesis that fish farming was indeed as profitable as they claimed. All the other farmers who had started before me and with me folded up business after multiple series of losses.

My postmortem analysis of my first loss identified all the things that could go wrong with this business. During the following three years, Agatha and I gradually addressed all the technicalities of the business. We hired the services of a consultant from the Water Research Institute, Emmanuel. Agatha went to the institute for a three-month course on fish breeding. Gradually we constructed our own hatchery, which is the bottleneck of any fish farm, and increased our number of cages according to need. This process was capital intensive, and in an industry where there were no loans or grants, it became very daunting.

Make no mistake: fish farms make money, and our advisers were right. What was essential were technical know-how and financial backup. At the time of writing this memoir, we are in our fourth year of business, and Volta Tilapia Limited has eleven employees feeding Ghana's population with about ten thousand tons of tilapia per month. The company is now self-sustaining and is reinvesting its profits in expansion. The company aims to own its fish-feed processing plant in the near future and multiple cold stores in the major cities for distribution and to become a leading contender in the tilapia business.

Being a doctor is great. You have the comfort of a good living as long as you work. What if you still want to have a good living without too much work? It's possible, but you have to work your whole life to save enough money first. What if something happens to you and you cannot work long enough to save that money? Then what?

These thoughts taunted me from the earlier years of my medical career. A bit of a business diversion from medicine in the form of real estate appealed to me. Owning a chain of hotels crystallized into my dream. As I battled with these ideas, I woke up one morning with bad news from London. One of our medical school classmates had just passed. He went to bed in good health and did not wake up again. He was a prominent gynecologist in a leading hospital in London. Molerh was his nickname. With a very likable and magnetic personality, he had organized all our classmate reunions. Six months before he passed, he had organized the biggest reunion in Orlando, Florida.

While I was coming back from his funeral, thoughts of his sudden death ignited my dreams, and I made my decision. So I set sail to realize this dream.

Anyone would tell you that dreaming of owning a chain of hotels from nothing is grandiosity. But this is not a delusion if you were born into a very wealthy family. All you would have to do is ask your dad at the dining table for $5 million of capital, and he would write you a check the next morning. It is that simple. But what if you have no parent with such an exuberance of wealth? That would be called delusions of grandeur.

There are people who want to see their bank accounts overflowing with money before they do anything, and others jump into it with whatever they have currently. I am the latter. Doing nothing is not an achievement, but doing something is, however small. The dogma that the rich get richer and the poor get poorer is true in all its senses. It is because the rich initially did something small and are able to use the small thing to do bigger things.

My inherent financial planning to achieve a goal is to set it up in three categories: short-term, medium-term, and long-term. This hotel idea is a long-term goal, and it is set up to take about ten years to get my first one built. The short- and medium-term investments fuel the long-term goal.

Instead of putting money away in a bank's savings account, I used it to start building a fifty-room hotel one block at a time. I am also making use of my short- and medium-term investments to fuel the long-term investment. If it takes me ten years to do it, I will have achieved my goal. To build the second and third hotels is much easier than building the first one. You now have clout, and financial people will start listening to you.

As I write this memoir, I am very close to the completion of the first hotel.

Chapter 14

ROMANCE

Adolescence is a very challenging period of life as one transitions from child-hood to adulthood. It is the years when there is an outburst of hormonal changes in the body, leading to the final body habitus and sexual development. During these changes, the brain, also undergoing growth, is too immature to comprehend what is going on with the body and requires a lot of guidance. Parental guidance is crucial during this challenging time of growth.

Unfortunately, a lot of families fail to provide their kids with the necessary education and allow them to explore these challenging times on their own. Teenagers are left alone to explore their own sexuality, sometimes to their detriment. I have come across many young female students who were caught in surprising and embarrassing accidents at school because they did not know about the menstrual cycle.

Teenage pregnancies were very common in the village. Since there was no social safety programs and family support, a lot of these girls dropped out of school. Many of these girls were lured to the Ivory Coast and Nigeria and sold as sex slaves. They returned many years later to the village and succumbed to AIDS and hepatitis.

Exposure to various forms of STDs leads to damage to the pelvic structure in girls, resulting in an inability to have children. Barrenness in this society was considered a great taboo and was usually attributed to some external spiritual force. It was not uncommon to say it was because of the work of witchcraft of a close family member.

For males, obstruction of the urine outflow pipe was common late in life because of scarring from repeated gonorrheal infection. I witnessed many of these reconstruction surgeries during my medical training.

In short, sex education was never taught—at least in my family. This is a very important subject in one's upbringing that, in my opinion, many Ghanaian families feel uncomfortable addressing. My sex education was acquired from a mate the same age as me called Opo T.

Opo T was brought up in the city of Accra. His family relocated to the village during our teenage years. We were both fortunate to be in secondary school at the time we met, and since this was a rarity in the village, we clicked immediately. We were both in boarding school, but we spent our school breaks together in the village. He was a prominent character in the village because he spoke better English and was taller, muscular, fair in complexion, and a great soccer player. His family and my family had a common lineage, and that created a strong brotherly bond between us.

By virtue of Opo T's physique, city-boy status, and reputation as a great footballer, he immediately won the admiration of all age groups, including the young girls. But Opo T, coming from a literate family and the city, was clearly well cultured in that area. He enlightened us on sex education, safety, pregnancy, and its consequences. I chalked him up as my sex education teacher, and with his guidance, we navigated this treacherous path of immature brains trying to grope a diseased world, which had befallen many of our contemporaries. Opo T and I came out unscathed. Today, we are inseparable, great pals. Opo T rapidly went through the ranks of Ghana customs after his university education, and he is marked to be the next head of Ghana customs at the right time.

I met my first love, Mabel, in the village. Strange as it may be, she was Opo T's cousin. Her mother also relocated to the village since she was one of the fortunate ones to be in a secondary school. She was very attractive, studious, and exceptionally multilingual. Just as one would with a first love, I wanted to be with this person forever. That was how it felt. But the whispers of the family undertones soon became louder and louder.

"How could you marry your cousin?" was yelled out eventually. Hearing this for the first time was like a knife going through my heart. We were both devastated that even though we loved each other, the family was going to be in our way. That dampened our spirits and marked the beginning of the end of a first-found love. Many years later, Mabel married a policeman in the village, with whom she had a child. Mabel died a few years ago in her forties in line with the low life expectancy in the village.

As a studious boy growing up, I had set up expectations for myself. I wanted to be a doctor and a businessman. The only impediment in my way was me. Throughout my life, I have been guided by this principle that I am the only one who can fail myself. As a result, I have been able to maintain a focused posture and have the ability to train myself as to what is important and what can wait. Nobody could lure me away from my laser focus to self-fulfillment.

I am attracted to most women, and I have no difficulty meeting or befriending a female. But I was able to tell myself that all that could wait until I had achieved my goal and that when I achieved my goal, I could have anyone I wanted. I selfishly removed anyone who was a distraction in achieving my set goals. This principle has guided me to stay on course, and I have proved myself right.

I was ready to take on the responsibility of a girlfriend when I was two years from becoming a doctor. It was my fifth year of medical school. I was vacationing in the village and went to the next major town, Koforidua, to run some errands. While on the errand, I went to a restaurant in the next big town to have a bite. The girl who served me was also a student helping her mother. When I asked her name, she said Nana Akua but to call her Adeline. As it was, it was very flattering to call someone by her English name. So it was the beginning of what I expected to be a long-haul relationship. We had a traditional marriage two years later, just before I graduated medical school. It was all very nice and glorious.

During my internship, the hospital provided me with an accommodation. It was a one-bedroom apartment. Being a village boy with a one-bedroom apartment in the city provided by the government free of charge was a very laudable achievement, and the pride on the faces of my family when they visited was immeasurable.

I moved into this new kingdom with my new wife, Adeline. It was the beginning of a new journey of cohabitation with a permanent lifelong partner, two young people living in a world that was difficult to disentangle from our culturally acceptable extended family system—a system that is sustainable because of its buffering medium that edges off extreme suffering by providing social security for its members. The members of the family ensured that they passed on the benefits they enjoyed to the less fortunate. Anyone who deviated from this norm was considered ungrateful.

With this frame of mind, we received family members in our new abode with open hearts; all they wanted to see was how good we were living. We entertained them with dinners and drinks. They left contented in their hearts with thoughts that I had finally arrived.

During this period of my new life, when I began to see clearly the direction of my future, I extended an olive branch to my sister, Mamle, whose money I had used for my previously failed business ventures. She had given birth to a baby boy. The boy's father absconded after his son was born. This boy, seven years of age, was caught in the quagmire of our exodus from the village to the city. He found himself crowded in the housing I provided for them with few prospects for a good education.

This boy, called Awah, was named after our great-grandfather, "the Warrior." I sensed he would have great potential if given the right foundation. With the permission of my new wife, I brought him to live with us so that I could give him a good basic education. It was also to reciprocate the favor my sister had done for me during my hard times.

Everything was really going well in the beginning, but soon I began to notice a change of character in my wife. The usual cordial reception of my family members changed. When they visited this time, she would leave the house. Her mother commented one time that my family should seek permission before visiting. The small boy, Awah, became a constant target of harassment. He would come back from school and cry all afternoon. My wife accused him of shouting insults at her in my absence, which the boy, amid crying, would deny. Her family encouraged her to get rid of the boy because he could be my secret son. My wife was acting on the wishes of her family.

Then one of her sisters reminded us that we were both sickle cell carriers and that we should not even be having kids together. Sickle disease ravaged my family, causing early deaths in affected children. I will discuss this in the chapter about sickle cell disease.

In the midst of this confusion and frustration, Adeline became pregnant with our first child. A baby girl was stillborn. It was a very strange circumstance for a pregnancy monitored from beginning to term, and within a few hours of delivery, the baby came out dead. It was shocking to me and very strange.

As the turbulence of the marriage continued, I became hooked on sleeping pills. I was my own prescriber, and I rapidly escalated to higher doses because the previous dose did not work.

I eventually moved the little boy out of my home and placed him with his mother on the other side of town, about ten miles away. Since it was the middle of the school year, I could not change the school. I picked him up every morning for school near me and drove him back home after school. Many times I encountered near accidents because I was hooked on sleeping pills but still exhausted from lack of sleep.

The relocation of the boy solved that problem but did not solve the problem of my family visiting. The boy narrated what had happened to him to his mother, and my whole family got wind of it. This started a fight between the two families.

One day my ace friend Opo T, who was then a young customs officer, visited. His little boy, Mate, was sick, and he wanted me to help him. When he left, Adeline told me I should not talk to him any longer because Opo T was bad-mouthing me. She further asked me not to confront him either.

Many weeks passed when I bore this grudge against Opo T. Then, one day when he visited again, I decided to ask him about what Adeline had said about him. Opo T is a tough guy who never cries. But that day he wept like a baby in disbelief at such an accusation. Adeline did not respond.

When Opo T left, the two of us prayed over it to address our problems. But the family influence on Adeline regarding how the marriage should be was too strong. We tried to kick-start the relationship by having a small-scale church wedding, to which we invited fewer than five people.

She became pregnant with a second child, Ed. At this time, I was ready to pursue my postgraduate training in England. So I left Ghana. The child was born in my absence. My family performed the naming ceremony.

The peace I experienced after I left the shores of Ghana did not give me the appetite to ask Adeline to join me in England. I decided this should be my new normal, and it was time to move on with my career trajectory. Remotely I took care of my baby boy, Ed, who is today two years away from becoming a medical doctor in the United States.

After a few years, my clinical rotations took me to a small town called Abergavenny in Wales. This is a region of Great Britain located on its western border and the home of a great rugby team, the Dragons. It was the coal mining nerve center of Great Britain, but the emergence of clean energy collapsed the industry, rendering many of its citizens unemployed. The first impression one would experience in Wales is about their funny English accents, which, when you are accustomed to it, would make you identify any Welshman in any part of the world. They have their own language, Welsh, which was being revived after many years of suppression by the English. At the time, the sentiment of the Welsh was that they were getting the short end of the stick by being part of Great Britain, and their politicians were voted in with the unexpressed mandate to level the playing field. It was therefore an enormous source of pride for the Welsh to see their great scholar and politician Neil Kinock, notable for his very long winding sentences and verbosities, as head of the Labor Party, face up in the British Parliament against Margaret Thatcher, the Iron Lady.

I was the only black man in this small town, but the great welcoming hearts of the Welsh were like none that I had ever experienced before.

I was rotating in chest medicine as a senior house officer, treating their sick people, a lot of whom were afflicted with end-stage lung disease as a consequence of years of coal mining and excessive smoking. It was during this intense work that I ran into a Welsh girl, Linda, on the medical floor. I was available, and she was also looking. When two people have the same agenda, nothing else matters. So we rolled and became the talk of the town. Two years later, we were married.

The thing that bothered me in the beginning about Linda was her unpredictable anger and lack of its management. It was expressed in its many raw forms irrespective of place. She also easily got panicked in simple situations to the extent that she was scared to drive even though she had her driver's license. She was very picky about little things and easily complained when things were not put together in certain ways.

By nature, I am thrilled by challenges and malleable to stress, and my breaking point is about 260 degrees, above which I would begin to reconsider my options. And this was her gold mine. Many men would have given up on her when I tried to navigate her through personal therapy. I resorted to my well-known mantra that if no one is dead in any situation, it can be fixed. I took a lot of verbal beating in the process, but I felt rewarded when her mother commended me for being the only man who could marry her daughter.

But people get along in any relationship when they focus on their good sides rather than their bad sides. Linda was a typical British-groomed woman who took after many of her parents' values. She was not wasteful and was always conscientious of putting money away for the future. To this extent, she would save money rather than use it on expensive clothing. I had to make her spend money on herself. This agreed with my own commitment that I would never want to see the face of poverty again, and I would live for tomorrow rather than today.

She was very adaptable to any culture, and she was able to cook many African dishes. She kept the home so orderly that any disruption led to rapid, uncontrolled reprimand.

With the help of her parents, I was able to get through the tedious visa protocol that enabled my paralyzed mother, accompanied by my sister Atta, to come to Great Britain for a cure. Linda fell short when my mother was going through her recovery to walk again. She became intolerant to their living with us. She would understandably take a weekend break from us, but she made them feel unwanted by quickly pointing out their infringement.

One summer afternoon, we came back from shopping and found Linda with our twelve-inch television set in her hands climbing through the window. Her explanation was that it was to demonstrate how a thief could have stolen our only TV set because we had left the window open. It was understandable that we felt that this was extreme and weird.

It was difficult for Linda to have a normal conception, so we had to resort to in vitro fertilization. After many tries, which cost us a fortune, we were blessed with a priceless, precious daughter, Lianne.

When I made up my mind to come to the United States to continue my dream's journey, Linda was not on board with the idea. She did not think relocating from Britain would offer her any benefit. When I explained the benefits she would derive, she complied, and together we made the move.

She was a good mother to my kids, whom she raised with the strictness of her British upbringing. I chalked up many successes while we were together in education and in business. What kept me going in this relationship was my inherent ability to be malleable in stressful conditions and to bend backward to about 270 degrees to absorb shock. I was also committed to fathering my kids in the relationship until they were at least eighteen years old. Even though I made it look nice and glorious on the outside, the temper tantrums persisted and were unpredictable.

As a rice eater, I was ashamed to be reprimanded for accidentally dropping a grain of cooked rice on the floor, and the pettiness of this nature made my home unpleasant to live in. When my patience was exhausted over this pettiness, after many similar incidents, I made up my mind that the Rubicon had been crossed, but I would wait for my youngest child to reach eighteen years of age before moving on. I made it obvious that I was no longer part of these shenanigans.

Then, one early morning, during the period when I was preparing for my medical recertification examination, the doorbell rang, and I answered. It was the police serving me a divorce notice from Linda. My first question was why she did not give me a heads-up beforehand, and the second feeling was big relief. Then, sheepishly, I decided that even if we divorced, I would still live in the house because of Lianne, who was still very young. My dreams were short-lived when another court order came saying I needed to vacate the house.

Suffice it to state here that by nature, my heart has been engineered never to be broken. No human can give me a broken heart, and I would never put my hand on my head and sob for a broken heart. I see that as weakness on my part to succumb to minor bumps in the road, and it has helped my course of resilience. I was able to prepare for the examination during this turbulent time and passed with success, albeit with effort this time around. After a long costly battle in court, we were finally divorced—to my great relief.

Michele was assigned to my office as a project manager from her medical software company to work on the implementation process of our electronic medical record system. It was there that our eyes met. Since she was available and I had just emerged into the market, it was not difficult to bond. It was during the time of the difficult, turbulent, and costly divorce process that she offered me a great deal of support.

Michele is a Canadian and hails from a relatively small town called Halifax. I had previously associated this name to an airline disaster that occurred close to its coast many years before when I was living in England. Little did I know that the name stuck in my head for the good reason that my future spouse was going to originate from its bosom. This northeastern coastal town in Canada, despite its small size, has seen the glory of many industries, including pharmaceuticals. Its fishing industry particularly interested me as it stimulated my own fish farming activities in a quest to feed the nation of Ghana.

Michele's mother is a French speaker from Montreal. Her biological dad was British. He succumbed to the ills of cancer when Michele was four years old. This left Michele with a huge void in her life from which she occasionally got flashbacks.

Michele's stepdad, Rick, responsibly took the helm of a fatherly figure to raise her and her sister, Claudia. The perfection of Rick's responsibility is such that an outsider would never be able to tell that the two girls were not his biological children.

Her mother's French is typical of Canadian French. Being a French scholar who speaks France's French, I was very excited to communicate with the mother in French. The difference between the two French dialects is similar to having a conversation in English with someone from Scotland. Even though the words are the same, the differences in the emphasis on the consonants are difficult to instantly recognize and make communication very difficult. The difficulty of Canadian French is well known, and my French professor gave instances where their speech sometimes had to be subtitled in France to be understood.

Michele never experienced poverty to the extent that I did. She never faced a day growing up of wondering where the next meal would come from. Comparatively, she lived a rich life. This subtle difference in upbringing has magnified the different ways the two of us see life as adults. My modus operandi is that having faced raw poverty while growing up, I do not want to relive it ever again, and my activities are geared to conserve for tomorrow. Therefore, I am cautiously more conservative than she is.

Canadians are generous people and welcome everyone. Michele often brands them as always wanting to have fun. I disagree with this broad generalization of Canadians, and my own judgment of them is typified by the gesture of their current prime minister, Justin Trudeau, in allowing the mass assimilation of refugees in their country. This is the summation of who Canadians are.

Michele and I got married after two years of knowing each other. Her first pregnancy was terminated because of a genetic defect discovered in the womb during the fourth month that would have made the baby developmentally challenged. The second pregnancy was genetically perfected by artificial selection of the best embryo through in vitro fertilization, leading to the birth of another precious princess, a leftie, Ama Karley Rose, the first and only grandchild of Michele's parents.

Like Linda, Michele has certain characteristics that I like and others that I do not. But focusing on her good qualities, they are far more than I could have imagined. She has a carbon copy of my big laugh and is an engine of extreme efficiency. Provide a job outline to Michele, and it is done with speed and accuracy. This commonality has given tenacity to our union. Michele is fun, and being a good mother with a loving heart provides a welcoming home to all my kids. She has her own sense of purpose and a set of dreams she wishes to pursue.

Not surprising for two people from different worlds meeting in the land of opportunity, there are many cultural differences that we have to contend with. Navigating through such differences and ironing out the bumps make our marriage very exciting and cohesive. So far we have been married for five years and counting.

Chapter 15

KIDS

I have three biological kids: Skin, Chipmunk, and Small Chipmunk. It would be incomplete not to add my nephew Awah as my first adopted child.

Awah is the house name given to Robert, who was the firstborn of my sister Mamle. He is like one of the many children abandoned by their irresponsible fathers. Many such children have come to surprise their absentee fathers years down the line, and such is the path of this boy, whose potential I discovered when he was only seven years old.

As a return of a favor to my sister, whose money I first used to test my bumpy road of business failures and successes, I decided to take care of her son's education and health and release him when he was able to look after himself. So when he was seven, I took him under my wing. I took him to my first home to school him. This turned out to be a turbulent disaster for him as my first wife disappointingly rejected him.

Notwithstanding, I was able to remotely look after him financially and emotionally after I returned him to his mother. Being a child who needed a fatherly role model in his life, he took after me and emulated my studiousness and tenacity. He did not falter with his education and achieved as much as he could. He had big dreams of what he wanted to become and diligently worked for it.

He managed to complete all of his basic education in Ghana and was able to gain admission to pursue a college degree in the United States. Throughout his education in the United States, I supported him financially and emotionally until he graduated at the top of his class with a bachelor's degree in construction management.

He turned down many job offers after graduation and went into business. He is currently running a successful health-care business and, more importantly, has not forgotten his roots. He is helping to support the extended family system in Ghana by taking care of their educational and health needs.

He is blessed with a good wife, Ruth, and a beautiful daughter, Brielle. He is mindful of his past experiences and is grateful to God. With the help of his pastor and Prophet Mamie Angie, he has paid me back in many ways for the good things that have done for him.

Skin was born in Ghana to my first wife, Adeline. He was born when I was in London pursuing postgraduate studies. My family, as per the custom, performed the naming ceremony. He was named after my great-grandparent Edward Christian Edmond. However, during his early upbringing by his mother and the prevailing discontent between the two families, her mother's family decided to call him Nana Yaw.

With my support, the mother took good care of him in his early infancy in Ghana. When he was about five years old, his mother left him in the care of her family in Burma Camp, the military residence for Ghana army officers in Accra. She went to London to live and pursue nursing training; at this time, I relocated to the United States for further postgraduate studies. I continued to send support to his mother's family in Ghana. However, when I visited Ghana and wanted to take my son out, her family refused to let me. The uncle with whom he was staying was a military officer and threatened to have me arrested if I took him out of the boundaries of the house. So without any court order, it was like a supervised visit for a couple of hours each time.

What was surprising to me, despite the financial support I provided, was how skinny and bony the boy looked. Luckily, he was put in a very good school, and his academic standard was above average. After several such visits, I decided to get custody of him and bring him to the United States. This was not difficult in light of an absentee mother and a willing father.

During my second-year residency, he joined me in Chicago. I did not know how best to call him other than to address his obvious thin physique that earned him the name Skin. Besides his thin physique that made him look much smaller than the American kids his age, he was way ahead of his class academically in the public school in Hillside, Chicago. He sailed through school and caused absolutely no trouble. He played the saxophone and joined the Boy Scouts, and I participated with him in tae kwon do class. As a boy, Skin showed himself grateful to have me in his life. When he visited me in the hospital and I would be in my white coat, he would run to hug me. He always wanted to imitate me in many ways. He wanted to wear vision-correction spectacles like I did to the extent that he feigned vision impairment as a child. The optician quickly recognized the inconsistencies during the eye evaluation and, with my consent, provided him with placebo eyeglasses. This solved the problem immediately. After a couple of years, he quickly recognized the inconvenience of the eye-wear during sporting activities, which he enjoyed so much. He also noticed the little difference the glasses made in his visual acuity. Then, gradually, the fun of wearing eyeglasses wore off, and his eye became normal again.

Skin was a great athlete. He started off with American football but had two injuries resulting in two broken bones. He gave up and took to hurdles. He won many races and was almost recruited for the Ghana Olympic team but for a few technicalities on the Ghana side.

Skin scaled through his junior-year schools as an exemplary child and gained a full scholarship to attend a four-year college in Iowa. He graduated with honors in biological science.

After graduation, he worked as a laboratory technician and an ambulance technician while preparing for his MCAT examination to gain admission to a medical school. He was successful in his quest, and he is currently two years away from becoming a full-fledged medical doctor at the University of Illinois.

Lianne was a miracle baby. She flew cargo division of Air India in a frozen jacket before she was born. I believe this has something to do with her toughness, resilience, and self-determination of who she wants to be. She was and still is the first grandchild of Linda's parents, whose son, Edwin, gave no indication that he would ever get married. Lianne was highly valued, particularly in the light that she was unable to conceive naturally.

In vitro fertilization was the solution for not being able to have a baby by natural conception. Linda underwent the stimulation, egg harvesting, and fertilization in Wales. All the embryos were frozen. Two rounds of transferring embryos did not yield any result in Wales. Then it was time for us to relocate to the United States. After settling in Chicago, we decided to give it a go at having a child again. We had only one embryo left in the freezer in Wales. All the airlines declined to transport the frozen embryo to Chicago. Air India was the savior—with a price tag and bureaucracy—but the final result justified the entire initial predicament.

The single embryo took immediately with vigor in the land of opportunity and quickly marked all the nine-month milestones with ease and integrity. She was born by cesarean as a precaution and named after her two grandmothers, Theresa Margaret, but chose to be called her mother's abrogated name, Linda Anne.

Lianne was a crazily pretty biracial baby, chocolate colored with curly black hair and big brown eyes. She was full of life and vigor, and as she developed into a young child, she became readily noticeable and turned heads. Like most selected embryos, she was very healthy and chalked up all the childhood milestones as expected.

Being the first and only grandchild of her grandparents, she was showered with an overabundance of gifts. As a minimalist, I vehemently protested the magnitude of gifts showered on her by her grandparents, and on many occasions I deprived her of the excess and gave them to charity.

Lianne inherited all my African genes in looks and intellect. She would have been my clone if she were a boy. Her physique was unmistakably from any of my relatives in Ghana. I discovered her academic prowess when she was about three years old. Her mother read to her every night, and within a week, she would take the book and read it from cover to cover. She just memorized the pages.

Lianne was renamed Chipmunk at the age of four. One Christmas, after being dragged to the movie theater to watch my first kids' movie, *Finding Nemo*, I got into the groove and randomly rented another kids' movie, *Alvin and the Chipmunks at Christmas*. The movie was so entertaining that Lianne and I subsequently watched the whole series. After sitting through so much of this series, we started calling each other Chipmunk out of the blue. To this day, Chipmunk and I will be the first to watch any latest movie from Alvin and the Chipmunks.

We are still current, and even if Chipmunk gets married, I will call her to go and watch the latest Chipmunk movie.

Chipmunk ice skated throughout her youthful life. She perfected it and, with her team, won many competitions. She also competed in beauty pageants in Illinois and won many of those. She was fascinated by acting, and we provided her with the necessary education during her childhood. She played many leading roles. She was picked up by many agents who presented her for auditions in movies in Hollywood. As a young and upcoming actress, she participated in many paid advertising jobs and played minor roles in movies. She is on course to take the daunting steps to the pinnacle of movie stardom for the selected few one day.

Chipmunk also has a dual career path, which she decided on when she attained the age of fifteen. The teen years are a crucial, formative time in physique and intellect. This is also the period in school when the student manifests his or her strengths and weaknesses in the various areas of studies. It is helpful to choose a career path during this period in life.

At the moment, Chipmunk is seventeen, in high school, and flying high academically. Her strengths are in mathematics and sciences. She aims to combine business with medicine. Together, we have decided that she should be a dermatologist. This would be in tandem with her beauty business and acting career. Chipmunk is self-motivated like me. Unlike mine, her need is not money but guidance from her parents. Barring any surprises, she will attain her dreams.

Then comes my last baby of the family. She is only three years old. She is Ama, another chocolate-skinned beauty with long curly, bushy black hair. Already she is well ahead of herself in age and deeds. Confident and independent, she protests assistance in taking care of herself. Having not been to school yet, she already has good penmanship with her quirky left-handedness. She draws faces with big eyes and noses to represent her African heritage.

Like Chipmunk, the little one was also a product of in vitro fertilization. Her mother, Michele, having passed her prime of pregnancy, had her first successful pregnancy terminated at four months owing to the baby having Down syndrome. To mitigate this from happening again, we resorted to embryo selection. Michele's eggs were selected and fertilized in a test tube. The resulting embryos were biopsied to determine which ones were not carrying any genetic defects. Then two were transferred, and the product was one bouncy girl.

Michele was determined to give an African name to this little girl. Our names are based on the day of week that you are born or your position in the family. So it is easy for people to know the day of your birth or whether you are the first or the last born of the family. Therefore, after going through all the names available, Michele thought that Ama rhymed well with Awah. Ama is a name given to a Saturday-born girl. Therefore, she should have been born on that day to carry the name. We asked Michele's obstetrician if she could deliver the baby on a Saturday. She felt this was too much to ask for a name's sake.

Ama was born on a Thursday, so her name should have been Yaa. Michele was adamant about keeping the name Ama and said Yaa would not suit the baby. We therefore had to go against our ancestors and break the naming rule. The discrepancy was revisited during the naming ceremony when it raised eyebrows. The elder, Fred Eddie Quartey, verbalized his outright objection. We had to pour a special libation to pacify our ancestors before he would accept the name for the child. Ama has now become unique for bearing the name of a day she was not born on.

In order to be in line with my micro family tradition of nicknaming my kids, Ama is now Small Chipmunk in preparation for her induction into the Chipmunk family. At the age of four, she will be subjected to the fun of watching all the Alvin and the Chipmunks movies.

Small Chipmunk has just started a preschool at Chicago Montessori. Such schools are designed for children like her who are well ahead of themselves, and they learn by copying older kids. Her elder sister, Chipmunk, attended a similar school and was reading before she went to first grade.

If I wind the clock forward to when my hair is all gray and neatly coifed into a low cut and I am enjoying my retirement age in my seventies, I can envision Small Chipmunk being the third doctor in the family, diligently making sure my vital signs are up to speed and remotely managing me through the perfection of the now emerging telemedicine. It's a scary thought but realistic.

Raising kids is a challenging feat and fun when all the stars are lined up in the right direction. Parental influence is the undercurrent and driving force that steers kids in certain directions.

I was fortunate to be given the opportunity to mentor kids in one of the South Side, Chicago, public schools. There I interviewed kids in their teens about their future career plans. I was stunned by the answers I got from most of them. A lot of them had already assumed myopic views of life and aimed too low right from the word "go." They verbalized becoming hairdressers and the like, while others wanted to join gangs. The rationale, I gathered, was that they wanted to become like their brothers, sisters, and parents, and they wanted to make money quickly. The ones who were aspiring to become teachers, lawyers, and doctors were very few, and they were the products of families with higher educations.

I believe our African cultural inheritance of extended family systems has mitigated some of these natural phenomena by steering kids away from becoming too much like the blend of their immediate families and instead encouraging them to adopt the flavor of the entire family.

Chapter 16

SICKLE CELL DISEASE

My family has been a victim of this terrible disease. It has taken the lives of too many young people and left a horrible stain. Poverty and ease of accessibility to the local herbalists and spiritualists have boomed the business of the latter while keeping the victims from exposure to modern medicine. Furthermore, a lack of education and parents' fatigue from caring for the afflicted with limited resources, coupled with the obvious day-and-night suffering of the helpless victims, have created a bad taste in the community to the extent that death is chosen as a better option.

Sickle cell disease is an inherited blood condition that causes reduction of healthy oxygen-carrying cells, called red blood cells, in the body. The normal red blood cells are round and malleable and are able to squeeze themselves through the smallest blood vessels in the body to deliver oxygen. The sickle cells are like crescents, similar to the moon just as it begins to appear. The cells of this nature are stiff and find it difficult to pass through the smallest blood vessels. They stick to the sides of the vessels and sometimes block them. They are constantly breaking down, and the bone marrow has to work harder to replenish them. The consequences of this simple defect in cells lead to a lack in the supply of oxygen to the vital organs in the body.

A person can carry the gene partially. Such people are called carriers. They are never sick from the disease. Or they can be considered full carriers of the gene. These are the ones who are constantly sick from it.

The disease is innocently passed on through the genes of affected parents, who are carriers to their kids. Depending on which of the parents has the gene, the child can have the full expression of the disease or be just another carrier. The full carriers are called, in lay terms, sicklers. During my time in the village, they never reached reproductive age.

By genetic permutation, when both parents are partial carriers, there is the chance that among four children, one will be a full carrier, one will be normal, and the other two will be partial carriers. When only one parent is a partial carrier, then among the four children, there is the chance that two will be normal and two will be partial carriers. If the sickler, who is a full carrier, reaches reproductive age and marries a partial carrier, then among their four children, there is the chance that two will be sicklers and two will be partial carriers. Lastly, if a partial carrier marries a noncarrier, then there is the chance that two out the four kids will be partial carriers and the other two will be normal.

When afflicted by the disease in its full form, the sickler will exhibit many symptoms. These symptoms are also sickening to the helpless parents who look on, waiting for the inevitable to happen. Unexplained episodes of pain in the chest, belly, bones, and joints presented a lot of challenges in the village, where the strongest pain medicine was Tylenol. Helpless victims were left to suffer through this pain until it naturally abated.

Repeated breakdown of the red blood cells leads to a yellow tinge to the skin and eyes. The resultant anemia makes them look pale and weak. The villagers associated sicklers with physical weakness, and for this reason they are spared from performing hard labor on the farm and chores at home. There is clear evidence of delayed growth in the affected children, and they are usually smaller than their peers. This is a nasty stigma that is unfortunately extended to other children who, for one reason or another, are small for their age and got wrongly labeled as sicklers.

Nonhealing leg ulcers are very common in sicklers. To compound the difficulty of hard-to-heal ulcers, there was the practice in the village that all ulcers must be cleaned with very hot water. The temperature of the water was dependent on how much the victim could take. Their rationale was that hot water killed germs on the wound. But science teaches us that hot water also cooks the new flesh that grows to cover the wound. So there was persistent destruction of new tissue that would grow to cover the wound, and the wounds were not healing.

The abundance of disease-carrying agents like flies and mosquitoes in the sickler community created a world of hell for these people. Already their disease-fighting ability had been compromised by self-destruction of their own spleens, the organ designed to remove infections from the body. The sickler was left without a defense, just like a soldier without ammunition being attacked by enemies on the battlefield. These insects transmit various illnesses to the defenseless sicklers, who are therefore known to always be very sick.

The worst symptoms that one did not wish on anyone in a community without social help from the central government were blindness and strokes that the sickler sometimes faced. Even in the best of situations, caring for stroke victims could be very challenging. I have seen young sicklers suffer strokes and develop pressure sores from sleeping on concrete floors, abandoned at the compound of the spiritual healer to perform miracles.

Whereas in modern medicine there is no known medication to cure the victim of this terrible disease, there are management protocols designed to improve their quality of life. Most times these protocols improve their life expectancy from the deplorable ten years in the village to well into the late forties with modern medicine. The sickler in the village was left at the mercy of the herbalists and spiritual healers to provide a cure. The latter proudly accepted the confidence entrusted to them and took the afflicted through all the believed rituals of cure. Some of the afflicted met their deaths from the rituals.

The herbalists used concoctions of various herbal preparations known only to them. The route of administration was either through the skin or the mouth or by enema. One can immediately foresee the problems that could arise. I have witnessed victims who collapsed and died miserably soon after having enemas with these herbal preparations. There was no accountability for prescribing the wrong dose or the wrong herb.

Mutilating incisions of the various parts of the body were hallmarks of a chronically diseased person in the community, and sicklers were not spared this ordeal. The scary mutilations on the face were meant to discourage the spirits and devils from taking away the lives of scarred children. The incisions were also used as a portal of entry for the herbal concoctions. I witnessed skin infections that led to blood infections with dangerous bacteria and death as a result. I witnessed tetanus resulting from the inadvertent composite of the concoctions directly administered into these incisions.

Reflecting on this today gives me a sore heart to realize how we innocently presented our weakest and helpless children to their deaths in the honest conscience of trying to help them.

My mom was the partial carrier of the family. My father was not. I deduced this from the patterns of affliction in my family. No one did a blood test to determine their status with the disease. They all had the diagnosis of surprise. I was the only one who formally tested myself to know my status, and I am a partial carrier. So among my ten living siblings, four of us were partial carriers, and none was a sickler.

Knowing one's sickle cell status, though, would not have had any effect on the prevalence of the disease in the community. Lack of education, complacency, and doing things for the sake of love would have erased any benefit of knowledge that one had the gene. I typified the last group when I was reminded during the family feud that my first wife, Adeline, was a partial carrier. That did not deter us from continuing with our relationship. We took the chance to have Skin, who turned out to be a normal child.

Other members of my family were not so fortunate. My sister had a beautiful daughter. At the age of two, she became chronically jaundiced from the constant breakdown of the red blood cells. During the following five years, she exhibited most of the textbook symptoms of the disease. Her chronic bone aches kept us awake in the night. She moaned and groaned from pain, which was weathered with little pain medication. She had many visits to the herbalist, and that resulted in her fair share of the mutilating scars on her face, chest, and abdomen. These scars were more pronounced in the part of the body that experienced the most severe pain. One day when we woke up, the room was silent. She had passed away suddenly and quietly in her sleep as if to say she had had enough of this world. She was about seven years old. Mourners encouraged my sister to cheer up since the passing away had ended the suffering and she went to heaven. Just that was enough to console a broken heart.

Another sister, Mamle, had a baby boy. He also started having signs of the disease at the age of two. He was jaundiced all the time. He particularly had growth retardation. He was small for his age. He caught infections readily. He was not subjected to the treatments of the herbalist as much so did not suffer the wrath of the mutilating scars. My sister took him to the hospital at the slightest sign of any infection for which he was readily susceptible.

Soon the cost for the care of one child began to drain the family coffers. Signs of inadequate funds became apparent and were reflected in the lack of rapidity of seeking medical care. Soon this caught up with the boy, whose survival depended on so many medical resources. At the age of six years, he passed away after a brief illness. The usual thing was to accept death as a sad but better option over the suffering of a helpless child. Sick children are a nightmare for any parent, for one. But if you knew that sooner or later the child would perish because of the sickness, then it was even more heartbreaking for the concerned parent.

The last sibling whose child is still suffering from the wrath of this disease is my younger brother Steven. Steven has three boys. The first one, Jeff, is in medical school, and then there is a ten-year-old, and the last one is eight years of age. All of them are always at the top of their respective classes in school. Steven is a very good father to his kids. He is an average bloke financially, but when it comes to the health and education of his kids, he would beat the bushes to get them what they wanted.

Their youngest brother who is always sick. He visits the hospital more often than them. He looks smaller than his age. They play video games together when he is well. Everything seems mundane. However, the expert eye would notice that the youngest brother, Richmond, has a perpetual tinge of jaundice and smallness in stature. He has a higher frequency of infections than his siblings but, thanks to the diligence of his dad and modern medicine, has never suffered any major crisis.

Fortunately, the youngest, Richmond, is under the care of my schoolmate, Dr. Ayisi, and he diagnosed him with sickle cell (SC) disease. He is a sickler, but it's a milder form.

There are two types of sicklers: the SS is more severe, and the SC is less severe. Without proper care, they all have bad outcomes. However, the SC ones, with good medical care, tend to have much better longevity.

The last one, Richard, is the epitome of good modern medicine. Never once would Steven ever entertain the idea of sending him to the herbalist or the spiritualist. He would never endure the mutilating knife of the herbalist. He is thriving, and with my assistance, there is no limitation to the medical care available to him. Any illness is attended to expeditiously.

Richard was born in the right era, after the exodus from the village, the period devoid of the villagers' influence that attributes any ill health to the act of the devil and whose redress is only through the release of the bondage by the herbalist, spiritualist, or juju man. Richard will chalk up his life's milestones designed by God for his condition. The Almighty has provided the conduit in the form of modern medicine. This conduit is the only way that guarantees longevity. Anyone afflicted by sickle cell disease who does not follow the path of modern medicine will perish before his or her time is up.

I have already observed a paradigm shift in the village as the mentality of the emerging young and more educated gradually dilutes that of the fading old and less educated. This shift is enhanced by the government's introduction of a national health-care insurance policy that makes health care available to all at a fraction of the cost. Today, the life of a sickler in the village is not as grim as it used to be.

Chapter 17

AFRICAN SUPERSTITIONS AND BELIEFS

Superstitions are unfounded and unproven beliefs in a community that are passed on from generation to generation. The source of these superstitions is usually vague and described by the impersonal subject "they." The believers can sometimes have so much conviction that they find it ridiculous for a third party not to share their beliefs. Beliefs are mental acceptance of and conviction of the truth, actuality, or validity of something. So superstitions can be beliefs, but beliefs are not necessarily superstitions.

As a pragmatic scientist, I am very biased against superstitions and beliefs in my community, but I will try to present this subject as objectively as I can and allow the reader to make a judgment.

Superstitions have their origins in ancient times. Life was very simple then. Facts and figures were not cross-checked as one would do in these modern days of the Internet and Google. Some bold mythical scholarship, like the Chinese feng shui, offered explanations for some of these beliefs. Some beliefs have persisted and perpetuated because ancient rulers used them to impose unchallenged commands on their subjects.

Across all parts of the world, all communities, all tribes, all villages, and all towns, there existed at one time or another superstitions that effected a change of behavior of a community. It is very interesting to note that a superstition in one part of the world could be perceived as a joke in another.

Baby and pregnancy beliefs are typical examples of European-origin super-stitions, such as how it is forbidden to buy clothing for the unborn child or tell anyone you are pregnant within the first three months. It appears strange to Europeans and Africans who hold these superstitions to notice that baby showers and announcements of pregnancy within the early days are part of the excitement of having a baby in North America.

Some beliefs will never die. Halloween is celebrated across Europe and North America. It is of Celtic origin and is celebrated on October 31. It marks the end of the season of the sun and the start of the season of darkness. It is believed to be the day that the evil spirits visit the earth. Among many associ-ated superstitions about this occasion is the taboo of traveling on Halloween night. Halloween is very commercialized, and a whole business industry has been built around it. The magnitude of the business around this superstition will send it into infinite perpetuity. Again, this is a belief that is not celebrated by Africans.

I do not find it offensive when beliefs are taken on their face values and do not lead an individual to self-harm or harm of others. But some beliefs that are taken literally can lead to bad outcomes in villages across Africa, particularly the little village where I originated. Some of these villages still hold on to their beliefs like in medieval times, when the ancient rulers imposed their unchal-lenged beliefs on their subjects. In these modern times in the villages, the juju men, witch doctors, and spiritualists use their powers to cajole the minds of the unchallenging, helpless subjects, instilling beliefs in them, offering services to mitigate the beliefs, and sending these beliefs into perpetuity.

The believers of this category are in the lower socioeconomic stratum and have a much lower education. Some of the villagers, like myself in the early years, were inundated with a number of beliefs when they were less educated and less wise, and as they gained more education, they began to realize how ridiculous the beliefs are. A few, however, steadfastly hold on to certain beliefs even after attaining the highest education.

Beliefs are mind-sets and attitudes that only the believer can change when he or she is ready. In a world where each individual is entitled to his or her opinion and beliefs, it is pointless to impose one's beliefs on another person.

Confrontations of this nature can have grave consequences that would far out-weigh the subject matter.

I have identified three types of beliefs in the community of my little village in Ghana. As much as I can easily enumerate the negative outcomes of these beliefs, I am unable to do the same with positive outcomes. I will give examples of the three categories in my ensuing narrative.

The first one is the belief associated with superstitions. These are associated with our ancestral worship of deities and the conviction that the devil has a hand in every bad event. It seems to me that this is a quicker way of solving problems of a complex nature. Names of little gods are not invoked in vain. In my Krobo community, being cursed in the name of a god called Nadum will send people into sleepless nights. Playing the Nadum drums is supposed to evoke thunder and lightning and is reserved for periods of crisis, like wars. The superstition about this god dares not to be tested, and the belief continues, the people accepting its power as is.

There is also a strong belief in the existence of dwarfs with special spiritual powers. Some villagers will point you to the exact location where they live. These are usually no-go areas in the thick of the forest. When people go miss-ing, it is very easy to assume that the dwarfs took them away. Sometimes some of these people reappear and claim the dwarfs gave them spiritual powers. No one has ever seen these dwarfs before, but if any outsider dares to question their existence, he or she could become a laughing stock of the local people.

The second category of beliefs is the one associated with a bad outcome of an experience. According to the village, for example, people with boils or abscesses should not visit the hospital. Often you would hear the elders say that people died after receiving injections for these conditions. The afflicted would then be scared to go near a medical doctor. As I learned medicine, I began try-ing to rationalize their assumption, and the only thing I can think of is that they had witnessed the allergic reaction associated with the medication. Back in the day, penicillin was the only antibiotic widely used for many infections, including boils. It is a known fact that many people experience severe allergic reactions to this medication. This sometimes can lead to death if not treated. It is easy to conceive that one such reaction in the village led to a bad outcome for a victim and immediately resulted in a wrong assumption. But this would have become a talking point that was imprinted on the minds of many people and passed on from generation to generation. The only choice left for treating this condition was an herbal treatment that sometimes led to many acceptable complications.

In the village, respect for the elderly was paramount, and when they spoke, no one dared challenge. So their false associations were easily passed on from generation to generation.

The third category of beliefs is the one instilled into people by others who claim they are able to see into the future. I do believe that there are people empowered by the Almighty to perform this function. But I am also wary of the ones who use psychological means to outwit others and instill in them a belief that will make them function in a different manner.

My village is known to attribute all deaths to the work of the devil. Being a physician, I find it hard to come to terms with this conviction. Anytime I hear such an attribution after a death, I always add sarcastically, "So no one dies naturally, then? How about the Europeans and the Asians?"

And I always get the same look and response: "You don't believe in anything; one day you will believe."

It is not uncommon to seek spiritual postmortem comfort rather than physical when someone passes away. The spiritualist or the witch doctor or the juju man becomes the go-to person. The family of the dead will pay a fee to consult these mediators, who will speak to the dead. The dead will narrate through the mediator the reason for his or her demise and if there is any redress.

I visited a village in Ghana where a funeral was being held for a twenty-year-old girl who had just passed away after a very short illness in the hospital. I was told that the doctors did not know what was wrong with the patient before she died. This is a story of a superstition of my first category, which in my opinion can have potentially grave consequences.

The village is Kpeve, a fish farming community on the Volta Lake in Ghana. I spend a few nights there on my vacations to enjoy the quiet and serene ambience. It is a sharp contrast from my life in Chicago, where driverless cars are even being considered to roam its streets. To the villager in Kpeve, Chicago appears to be basking in the year 2018

Being a physician of thirty years of experience, I have never seen any death whose cause can be attributed to spirits. When I was told that the deceased twenty-year-old had been killed by her own sister, I was all ears. Soon after the sudden demise of this young girl, the family, shocked, wanted to find out what had actually happened to cause her death. They went through the intermediary of the spiritualist to speak with the spirit of the dead. The spirit told them she had had a quarrel with the elder sister over a drying line in the house, and during the quarrel, the living sister cursed her. It was the curse that sent her to her death.

The family came back to accost the sister. She confessed that this was the story, but she thought the curse was innocuous and did not know that it would cause the death of her sister. She was very remorseful for the sad end of her sister and cried bitterly.

I would not judge how the family handled this true story that occurred in my presence. Different people will have varied opinions about this incident depending on their beliefs and which part of the world they come from. The whole village felt this case was handled in the appropriate manner, and they were satisfied with the cause of death.

With my background in this modern world, I can immediately see a lot of unanswered questions. Among many of the questions would be the competency of the doctors in the village hospital and the availability of resources at their disposal for them to be unable to determine what was wrong with the patient. I would also have sought a physical postmortem and forensic science analysis, if need be, to find out a medical cause of death.

In modern medicine, dying is difficult, and in such a situation of early death, it is important not to simply attribute it to a spiritual cause. When a natural cause of death can be detected, it could reveal a familial predisposed condition whose treatment would prevent a similar bad outcome in the living siblings.

It is clear that I am preaching to the choir in the so-called modern culture, but when you live and breathe the culture around you in this village, my analysis would be considered totally absurd.

Another belief that is still rampant in my village is the connotation of mental illness. This is an illness that is not taken to the hospital. Not uncommonly in the villages and town, one can observe schizophrenics roaming the streets. They are commonly described as "crazy." It is obvious that they have not taken a shower or bath since the inception of their illness. Their uncut hair is rolled in thick dirt. They dress in tattered clothes picked up from the refuse dump, and they feed on dirt and sometimes carcasses. They speak to themselves, and in most instances they are harmless. They carry their baggage along anywhere they go. They sleep in the streets and bushes and endure all the elements of the weather with very little help.

From ancient times, mental illness has been considered to be caused by bad spirits. Sufferers were sometimes considered possessed by the devil. The treatments were always some form of spiritual exorcism. During the dawn of medicine, when institutions were built to house the sufferers of mental illness, these establishments were located far away from the centers of towns. But since we cannot run away from our responsibilities, these towns have grown to engulf these institutions.

Today, many mental institutions are in the inner cities. In many countries, authorities provide means to diligently take care of these unfortunate ones. They are treated and returned to their homes with some form of normalcy.

This good care of the "crazy" in the modern world has not caught on in the villages that I know. Once you start acting funny, talking to yourself, and seeing things that do not exist, you are immediately stigmatized. You have caught the disease of the spirits. You lose your friends, and in some cases your family will disown you. If you are lucky, you will be taken to the witch doctor, spiritualist, or juju man. In most cases, you will be abandoned in these healing homes. The ones who are unlucky eventually leave home to roam the streets and fend for themselves. I have known of some of them eating food from the garbage or living off fruits and vegetables from the forest around them. This harsh and hard life leads to early death, after which their corpses will be sighted in the bushes and streets.

I knew a couple who lived in Italy for many years, and when the wife became crazy, the husband brought her home to Ghana and abandoned her with her family. This is definitely an act of irresponsibility sculptured out of the culture of superstition associated with mental illness.

In the healing houses for mental illness, the rituals of exorcism can be very harsh. The spiritualist will most likely starve the possessed by taking him or her through a series of fasting and prayers. The witch doctors will chain the possessed to a tree and beat the devil out of them literally. They end up with bruises and scars. These rituals continue until the crazy one absconds into the wilderness and faces an early demise.

I was brought up in the village with the conviction that mental illness was caused by bad spirits. It was when I started studying medicine that I became aware that this anomaly is because of a chemical derangement in the brain. Modern medicine has advanced so much that it should be a serious criminal offense not to offer current medicine to a relative who has a mental illness.

Analyzing the villager who has never been exposed to the world and the Ghanaian Italian who has been exposed to a modern world, there is a commonality in their respective beliefs. And this belief is a strong superstition that can definitely lead to a bad outcome. It does not matter whether one lives in a modern world. What matters most is the belief that one takes along.

Strokes and boils are among many more medical conditions plagued with the belief that the victim would have a bad outcome when treated in the hospital. The common mantra when someone is afflicted with such a condition is that they "are not hospital diseases." Some people will even cite examples of deaths that occurred when these conditions were taken to the hospital.

Even in the best of circumstances, strokes are difficult to treat. The villager has recognized this prognosis very quickly and has come to the unfortunate conclusion that only the witch doctor can treat the condition. The witch doctor may have taken advantage of the natural history of strokes—that one-third will recover despite what treatment is given—and magnified this natural progression as success.

The belief around boils stemmed from the possible severe allergic reaction to penicillin, which was the only antibiotic available in the early days. These reactions may have caused death and led to a bad taste in the mouths of family members who passed on their bad experience from generation to generation.

Beliefs about strokes and boils have minimal spiritual connotations, and changing the mind-sets of people regarding their management with education is relatively easy.

The third category of belief is exemplified by my personal experience in October 2016, when I had a confrontation with a spiritual leader in Ghana. I am aware that there are good churches and also bad ones. There are good pastors, and there are also bad pastors. Ghana is plagued with such a complex mixture of these pastors, and stories you hear about the performance of some of the bad churches can make one sick to the stomach. People are desperate, and all it takes is a little glimmer of hope pronounced by bad pastors to win such people to their side.

I have no reservation when these men and women of God use their powers to do good things. I have a problem when some of them use psychology to outwit their followers and make them do what they should not do. My experience with this pastor makes me worried about the people who have put their lives and beliefs in his hands.

I had an urgent call from one of my sisters, Atta, in Ghana to speak to her pastor. When I asked why, my sister said to me that I was going to return to Ghana within that month in my coffin. The pastor asked that I speak with him urgently for prayers to avert such a tragedy.

The day before, my sister went to her evangelical church, and during the worship, the pastor had a revelation. Then the pastor asked the congregation which of them had a brother living abroad by the name of John. In Ghana, the name John is so common that each of the last three presidents of that country had it as his first name.

My timid sister owned up in the congregation that her brother John lives in Chicago.

Then the pastor revealed to the congregation that instead of her brother arriving alive to Ghana in that year, he would be shot by a Jamaican and brought to Ghana in a box.

My sister was invited to a private consultation with the pastor, and amid prayer, it was revealed to her what she should do to avert this from happening. One of the things was for me to call the pastor for prayers over the phone. She was asked to do some fasting and meet certain requirement to the pastor to shame the devil. When I refused to call the pastor, my whole family in Ghana went berserk. I was inundated with so many calls from my family in Ghana to consult the pastor immediately. In order to appease my family and allay their fears of my premature demise, I called this pastor three days later.

As soon as I introduced myself, I was overwhelmed by the incessant speech and negativity of this man. I have never heard such an address regarding details of how I would be killed by a Jamaican man with a gun, how I would not see my family again, and how my family would come to the airport and see a box with my body instead of me in person. Then he went on to say I should buy twenty-one bottles of Communion wines and call him the following day for instructions on how to use them. Then, after the devil was disarmed, I should visit his church in Ghana for prayers of protection.

This man's address immediately gave me a flashback to my childhood when my mother had been told I was not going to see Christmas and she put me through the embarrassing ritual in the compound of a church in the little village. I felt like I had just had a brawl with Lucifer, who—dressed in his full regalia but bare-chested, with his characteristic long crooked nose and armed with his devilish wand—stood on top of a mountain and blasted me with his worst and last curse. It was like speaking to Satan instead of a pastor.

After allowing him to go on for about thirty minutes, I stopped him and told him he was full of BS. Out of respect for my sister, I did not hang up on him and allowed the address to end naturally after another fifteen minutes. He was trying to convince me that it had not been my own will to respond in the manner that I did but rather the work of the devil.

He called me the following day to ask if I had bought the communion wine. I told him I did not have time for that. He preached to me again at length about the wine. He called the following day again, and when he thought he was confronting a stone, he stopped calling.

Superstitions and beliefs in my village are deeply rooted. I would have been a preacher of such superstitions and beliefs had I remained in the village. Today, I am a scientist, and I am satisfied with my explanation of many occurrences in life. I am devoid of any of the die-hard beliefs the villagers exhibit. I am considered a total stranger when I find myself in a confrontation with my own people about such strong convictions. They believe I am crazy with my scientific mind, and I also feel the same about them. But to live in harmony, we respect one another's views, which should be left at that until we both recognize one day who is right.

Chapter 18

PHILANTHROPY

Life's successes can be measured in multiple ways depending on how one perceives success. It can be measured as educational achievement, money, work, or how many lives one has touched. I will measure one of my successes in the world of giving back and making a difference in someone's life.

I made a significant contribution to a not-for-profit organization called Our Chance International, based in New York. This organization raised money in the United States to provide free health care for the needy. The beneficiaries of this service have been poor countries or countries with disasters and wars. Ghana, Haiti, and Iraq are among the countries this organization has helped.

The organization has a team of doctors from the United States in the fields of ophthalmology, general surgery, and plastic surgery. We made two trips to Ghana in the late '90s and set up bases at 37 Military Hospital in Accra and Cape Coast General Hospital in the central region of Ghana.

The thrill of these trips is the joy in the faces of the people whose lives we have changed. Among some of these dramatic changes is restoring the eyesight of a blind person by a simple cataract surgery. Poverty and inadequate health personnel in some of these countries have allowed the age-related thickening of the eyes' lenses to progress to the point where they no longer allow light to penetrate the eyes. This eventually leads to loss of vision, and the only treatment available is surgical removal. Unfortunately, in Ghana, the villagers refer to this whitening of the eyes as *kooko* and resort to herbal treatment.

The joy from this rapid recovery of vision emerges when the patient returns to the clinic the day after the surgery and the bandage on the operated eye is removed. What they see first is a human face, which they have not seen in many years. Many of them break down into tears when their sore eyes make this discovery.

Cleft lips and cleft palates are mostly unseen in the Western world because they are treated in children's infancy. In Ghana, they appear not to be seen because those afflicted hide in the shadows. They are shy to show their faces to the world. They hide parts of their faces with clothing. They are socially isolated. They are psychologically downtrodden. With our team of plastic surgeons specialized to treat this condition, we went on the national TV with pictures of cleft palates and cleft lips. We called on families with the condition to show up for free treatment.

In a country with apparently unseen cleft palates and cleft lips, we were suddenly inundated with people of all ages with the condition. Our team, led by Dr. Drew Schnidt, patiently repaired this condition, allowing the afflicted to regain their self-dignity and smiles that they could not show all the years prior to the surgery.

Hernias are also rampant in Ghana. Just like cataracts of the eyes, they are also called kooko. This is a concept reinforced by the herbalist that you do not take these conditions to the hospital, saying they are best treated by herbal medicine. As a result of improper treatment, they tend to grow bigger and bigger. People die from it as a result of complications such as bowel obstruction. They are usually kept secret to the sufferer alone, whose only consolation is to feel sorry for him- or herself.

In one instance of a hernia patient whose scrotum grew to the size of a football, he presented to us to regain his dignity. His wife had left him because of the hernia, and his children likewise had abandoned him because of the shame of the huge mass in his pants. His walking had become so labored that he became confined to bed.

He was presented to our team in Cape Coast by neighbors who felt sorry for him. He was obviously unable to walk when we saw him. Our expert team of surgeons from Illinois Masonic Hospital in Chicago set out to work on him.

Within an hour, his bowels were pushed back into his belly, the huge hole in the wall of the abdomen was sealed with mesh, his scrotum regained its normal size, and his dignity was restored. His first statement was, "I can marry again," and he thanked us.

Our surgical team treated a wide range of conditions, including webbed fingers, webbed toes, head and neck tumors, and tissues growing from the corners of the eyes. Also importantly, throughout the period that the team worked in Ghana, we collaborated with the local doctors and trained them on the management of some of the complicated cases. This was equally important as you cannot put a price on knowledge that makes a difference in someone's life.

Our surgical team did not only provide free medical care that changed people's lives and transferred knowledge to local doctors from experts from the United States, but we also donated important medical equipment to these hospitals. On each trip, we had prior knowledge of their equipment needs in terms of the procedures we intended to carry out. We bought that equipment for our use and trained the local doctors on how to use it, and when the mission was over, we made the hospital take ownership of the equipment. Because of this, 37 Military Hospital in Accra and Cape Coast General Hospital in the central region of Ghana have been beneficiaries of sophisticated eye equipment.

Many times you go on medical missions and meet certain cases, and you say to yourself, "I wish this patient were in the United States; we could take care of this condition very easily." The conditions would be complicated, but with a surgical team that has a multiplicity of experts in a hospital setting that has upscale postoperative care, the condition could be managed with ease.

This is what happened with Princess and Abenaa from Cape Coast. Princess was about ten years old and was blind from corneal opacity. The story was that her schoolteacher had hit her in the eye with a broom. All she needed was a corneal transplant, and she could see again. Abenaa had a condition called neurofibromatosis, when the nerve tissues swell into multiple tumors all over the body. In Abenaa's case, the nerve tissue was growing from one eye socket like an elephant tusk, completely obliterating that eye. She was about sixteen years old, living in the shadows and ashamed to present her face to the world. During the only times she would come out of hiding, she would cover half her face with a piece of cloth.

When our team assessed these two cases, we decided the only way they could be treated was to bring them to the United States. After going through the necessary protocol, we managed to get them visas to the United States. Both of them underwent successful surgery at Illinois Masonic Hospital in Chicago. I was instrumental in their care in Chicago and raised money for them while they were there, and on their return to Ghana, I presented each of them with a good sum of money to start a new life.

Not all medical interventions have happy endings, and when this happens on a medical mission to help people, it is very heartbreaking. This happened to our team at Cape Coast General Hospital in Ghana. Our general surgical team had nothing but surgeons with over thirty years of experience. They were adept in their fields, which had become second nature to them, and selflessly put out their arms to help humankind. When in Ghana, we met a young man in his twenties with a football-size hernia; he had lost all his dignity because of this seemingly simple, curable problem. The surgeons had nothing but sympathy and wanted to do all they could to help him regain dignity and respect for the many remaining years ahead of him. But things did not go according to plan. He had a successful surgery to repair the huge hernia under a spinal anesthesia. At the end of our long day of surgery, we made routine ward rounds at about 7:00 p.m. before we went back to our camp.

When we got to this young man's bedside, he was bloated and sweating and was in silent distress. We immediately knew what was wrong with him. We rushed him back to the operating theater and opened his abdomen. One of the blood vessels that had been tied had become loose, and he had lost a lot of blood into his belly. This was identified and repaired successfully.

Then we returned him to the intensive care unit, which I was in charge of. This was an intensive care unit in name only, because it had just a heart monitor. What this young man needed was blood, and with a couple of medications to keep his pressure up for a few hours, he would have been fine. My long night began with frustration that the blood bank was not open twenty-four hours. When I finally got hold of the technician, I was disappointed to discover that they did not have a single pint of blood available. The only option was to contact the teaching hospital in Accra, which was 150 miles away. It involved an ambulance transport to either take the patient or a bit of his blood for matching for compatible blood. The hospital did not have a working ambulance.

When I exhausted all options, I was left with simple IV fluids and medications to support his blood pressure and allow the little amount of blood left in his system to supply the necessary oxygen to his vital organs. This was to buy time for the next day when we could get some blood donated for his use.

As expected, his organs began to fail, starting with his kidneys, despite all the team's heroic efforts. He passed away at noon the next day. A somber day came to cover the enthusiasm of our devoted and dedicated team. Our spirits were dampened. It was the worst moment of any medical mission I have ever done. We worked with the family and paid for all the expenses incurred for his funeral.

My two medical missions to the Philippines were a great joy to me. This is a country with a population of over one hundred million people spread over seven thousand islands. Traveling from one part of the country to the other typically involves the use of planes, cars, and boats. The people are very friendly, and I liken them to those in my home of Ghana in many ways. It is still a developing country, but the big cities are just like those of any of the developed countries. The remote villages do not have much, and health care is particularly needed.

What struck me in the Philippines when I visited the marketplace was the height of the typical Filipino. With my meager height of seventy inches, I would have been lost in a crowded American market. In the Philippines, at that packed market square, I was a giant. I was very happy to be able to see far above the heads of almost everyone in the market. It felt good to be able to do that; it was weird but fun.

The Calvary Church of Naperville, Chicago, composed the team of medical personnel. It was made up of internists, family doctors, dentists, pharmacists, and volunteers of varied backgrounds. I made two trips to the Philippines with this team in three years. Each time, we traveled to remote islands where medical care was much needed. On one occasion, a village was separated from the rest on the main island by a river with no bridge. The only option was to walk through the river or over a dancing footbridge. I chose the former as a safer option.

We provided free medical care and supplied free medicines. Age-related blurred vision is a serious disability that impairs elderly people's ability to read or see faces clearly. A lot of elderly Filipinos have developed this problem, and our team provided free reading glasses to fix it.

There was a striking need for dental care. Starting from ages two to adulthood, it is unimaginable how much lack of fluoride in the drinking water can affect teeth. Our team of dentists was overwhelmed by patients with decayed teeth. From morning until evening, they extracted decayed teeth from patients three years old all the way to the elderly. The local dentists recounted instances where they had had to fit dentures to kids as young as six in order to prevent malnutrition.

The reward we had from this service was the genuineness of their gratitude. The smiles of appreciation were heartwarming and living that memory makes me feel content that I have made a real impact on someone's life.

I have, over the years, sponsored many people in education. Dr. Janice Appiah was a beneficiary of my kindness. The sudden loss of her mother during the earlier years of her medical training in Ghana put a lot of strain on her family. Her dad, Dr. John Appiah, who was my role model and mentor, had supported me during my difficult times in medical training after I lost my dad. This, I thought, was payback time, and I was in good financial standing. I offered to support her financially, and I did that until she graduated from medical school.

But my biggest source of pride was the help I offered to Dr. Frimpong in Ghana. His problem mirrored mine, and I was very happy when he graduated from dental school in Ghana and sent me his graduation picture.

The story began when I was visiting my old schoolteacher from secondary school, Father Batsa. During the visit, he and another school colleague, Dr. Chawey, were discussing a medical student whose father had just passed away. It was obvious that the student had no one to help him pay the school fees for the remaining three years of his training. They were discussing how to raise the money.

After obtaining a few details, I told them the discussion should end there and that I would take on the full responsibility of his education until he graduated.

Later on, when I was introduced to the student, Frimpong, I told him I was in charge and that all he had to do was concentrate on his studies. With all financial burdens now off his shoulders, he studied in an atmosphere of tranquility and graduated with flying colors. I was proud to see him take his first job at 37 Military Hospital in Accra as a dentist.

Helping other people does not always go the way you intended it to. Some people need a little push with the pinkie; others need to be carried on your head. The story of Ernest is a sad one.

Ernest lived across the street from my house in Accra. He was about ten years old, and I was surprised and saddened when I found out that he could not read the book my six-year-old had read and given to me to donate to the orphanage. Ernest's mother was a widow and burdened with many children. She was a petty trader and could hardly make enough money to feed her children. One of her kids was caught in a failed armed robbery and killed by the local mob.

Ernest, at the age of ten, was aware of his circumstances and wanted to change the course of the family fate. He compared himself to my family members, who were more literate at his age. He showed his frustration by crying at his predicament.

This touched me. I approached his mother to offer my help, which she gladly accepted. I enrolled him in a local private primary school. I paid for school bus service, meals, uniforms, and tuition. I even scheduled my visits to Ghana to coincide with the Parent-Teacher Association meetings. I was actively involved to make sure he would turn out a good educated young man to save his family. At one point, he asked if he could use my last name instead of his. I told him I would be proud.

But I noticed during the second year that his performance slipped, and the teachers gave me a lot of complaints about multiple absences. When I confronted his mother, I found out a few problems. The mother would sometimes fail to wake him up, and he would miss the school bus. She would then ask him to walk to school and demand a refund from the school to supplement the household upkeep. He was not tied down to the house to study after school, and he would be all over town, running errands for the family. After not heeding the multiple warnings, I gave up on him in the fourth year, withdrew him from the expensive private school, placed him in the public school system, and made him the responsibility of the family.

I have made significant contributions to orphanages in Ghana. The orphanage in Begoro in the eastern region of Ghana has particularly benefited from my benevolence financially and materially. I made my high school–age son, Skin, spend one week of his vacation in this orphanage to mentor the children and help build a poultry farm. This had a two-pronged effect of also making my son appreciate how fortunate he was to be raised in the United States.

Education and health are the two most important catalysts in life upon which success is built. Both are easily accessible when one lives in the advanced world and are sometimes taken for granted. In some cases, these benefits are even abused.

Truancies in public schools in the Western world are commonplace, and I consider this a missed opportunity for success. Abuse of the health-care system in advanced countries is unfortunate, and some of these people do not know how fortunate they are to have this benefit at their disposal.

In a third-world country like Ghana, these resources are considered golden. I have come across many aspiring students who could not have further education because of lack of money. I have lost many friends who were brilliant but succumbed to treatable ailments as a result of the inability to afford medical care. I refuse to make any member of my family suffer from lack of these basic necessities. I single-handedly make necessities available to all members of my family by being financially responsible for their health care and education. This has allowed my family to blossom in a world full of opportunities that only those with the know-how and in good health can tap into.

Chapter 19

SETBACKS-HOW I SURVIVE THEM

There are many obstacles in life, but the perception of these obstacles is dependent on whether the individual is one who sees a glass half-full or half-empty. The former sees these obstacles as a bump in the road and moves on, while the latter may lament and use these as excuses for their shortcomings.

I would rather requalify an obstacle as a challenge since it gives me a positive vibration in my soul and creates a positive attitude of how to deal with it.

Like many people, I have had my fair share of setbacks in life. Mine were mainly restricted to business and life skills. My academic path has been almost devoid of bumps. But each and every one of my challenges has been used to improve myself.

Initially, when the challenge would surface, I would lament and feel sorry for myself, but a few months or years down the road, that same misfortune would turn into an advantage.

It was much later when I discovered that destiny was the big player in my life. As soon as I discovered destiny, I began to change my perception of life's challenges. My attitude and approach toward issues and problems in life has hence been fashioned such that as long as no one is dead, any problem can be surmounted, and everything is replaceable.

I am always guided by my philosophy that I will try to fly to the sun, and if I am unable to get there, I will still accomplish a great achievement by landing on

Mars. Goals that I set for myself may be somehow unrealistic, but I am always prepared for the outcome. A mediocre result is always better than doing nothing, and failure may just be destiny.

Taking business risks thrills me. I am open to trying something new even if I have no clue about it. However, I always have a safety mechanism for failure so that if I fall, it is not flat on my butt.

Not all things go according to plan. I learned that very early in my business career. A good businessperson must learn to adapt rapidly to changing terrains. It may look good on paper, but the real test is when the rubber meets the road.

To be born with a silver spoon in one's mouth would have been easier. You could have just got your dad to cut you a check, and that would have helped accomplish a dream in a year or two. But most people are not that fortunate. If all you have is you, then it requires a lot of strategy and planning.

Resorting to the basics of learning how to sit, then crawl, then walk, and then be able to run was my guide. Rushing through any of these always leads to disaster.

The lesson that I gained is that the business world is full of disappointment and upsets. One has to be careful when people start to lay out a business proposal with you. Talk is cheap. Always look beyond the cheap talk when discussing business proposals and promises. Consult and cross-check all proposals with yourself. What sounds too good to be true is always too good to be true. Money never comes cheap; otherwise, everyone would be rich.

Had all my plans been fulfilled, I would have been a Catholic priest and, with my fabric of business-mindedness and charity, grown the church to the point that I could have been a contender for the highest spiritual calling. Or I could have by now been an owner of multiple hospitals in America, a multimillionaire maybe, and in my backyard would have been a private jet and a yacht. Or I would have retired by now as a mining tycoon, owning a fleet of heavy earthmoving equipment. All these would have allowed an early kickoff of my real purpose in life, philanthropy.

But I am still here, being guided by destiny and obeying the basic principles of sit, crawl, walk, and run. And while not being able to land on the sun, I am hoping to land on Mars with flying colors.

Chapter 20

ACHIEVEMENTS

ACCOMPLISHED DOCTOR

I would humbly like to enumerate some of the contributions I have made to this world to make it a better place. I am aware that my contribution may be meager compared to other people's, but I am thankful the Almighty has given me the ability to leave a mark behind.

At the age of fifteen, I made up my mind to be a doctor. But I did not want to be an ordinary doctor; I wanted to be a doctor with a kind heart. Against all the odds that my origin presented, I have been able to weave through all the nuances to accomplish my childhood dream.

I am not proud of the daily routine of practicing this profession, which I consider a job. But I am proud of the heart I put into it, going to extremes to give extra life to people who would not have survived had I not been in their lives. This is the part that makes me feel not just like a doctor acting like a computer by making diagnoses and spitting out prescriptions but like a human with a kind heart whose touch, feel, and gaze transmit cure and comfort to a patient. Through these measures, I have touched many souls.

I will not dwell on my immediate family in Africa, who are enjoying extra bonus years on their life expectancies and defying all the statistics of the average life spans in Ghana, nor my mother, who gained over twenty extra years on her life expectancy before she died. All this happened because I am in their lives.

What I really want to dwell on are strangers whom I came across by accident and whose lives I changed by virtue of being a physician. I can recall many such instances, but I will just mention a sample.

The dewormer that saved a life is the one I always remember. I visited my village one Christmas when I was a young doctor attuned to tropical medicine. I was called to see a young child who was short of breath. After a brief history and examination, I figured out that he had Loeffler's syndrome. This is a medical condition where acute infestation of the body by certain worms leads to a severe lung reaction like an asthma attack. If not treated, it could lead to rapid death.

When physicians are faced with these situations in the middle of nowhere, it is like being called while flying in an airplane to treat someone with a heart attack. The physician would think of all the things he or she could do to treat such a patient then suddenly realize there is nothing to work with—just sit tight with the patient until the plane makes an emergency landing.

Remember that the villagers are poor, and there are no hospitals close by. In the situation I was confronted with, I would be financially responsible for any medical treatment I offered because they simply did not have any money. Whatever resources they had were spent to provide a decent once-a-year Christmas meal.

Had I not been there, they would have sought the help of the local herbalist or juju man. That would have certainly ended the child's life. What this patient needed was an appropriate dewormer, oxygen, hospitalization, and the whole nine yards of modern medicine. But thinking like this in such a situation was tantamount to having a sweet dream. What was available were a few drugstores located fourteen miles away.

So rather than acting like a computer and spitting out a prescription, I told the family I would be back in a few minutes. I drove the fourteen miles to the next city to look for a drugstore that carried the medication I had in mind to prescribe. After a few rounds of driving to drugstores, I was able to find the appropriate dewormer.

This was the only available solution to this conundrum, and I had to pray that it was sufficient to divert a potentially bad outcome. Our prayers were answered when, within two days, the child's condition stabilized, and on the third day, there was a clear sign that he would make it.

They may have considered me as their hero and the best Christmas present God had sent them. I was just being myself and my best presents were the smiles I put on their lips and the joy that sprang out of their souls in this festive time of year. It was a feeling that far surpassed any financial compensation I would have received.

Deep in my soul, I have a feeling that so many similar things I have done in my life are a way of refining Mr. Destiny to take me where he wants and continually reinforcing my conviction that the blessings that come my way are not just serendipity but a reaping of the seeds I have sown.

BUSINESS

Compared to medicine, my business successes are just amateur. Notwithstanding, I have chalked up many significant milestones that would at least land me on the red planet, Mars.

I have used my pitfalls in my business ventures to guide me, and I find myself cruising on an even keel to the goal I have set for myself. What really matters now is obeying the natural principle of sit, crawl, walk, and run and allowing time to turn the tide toward my destination.

After many years of trial and error, so to speak, two businesses are emerging as proof that I have not failed myself as a businessman. They are both at their walking stages of my principle, and when they begin to run, they will be a force to reckon with.

The first emerging business venture is a fish farm. I am intrigued by challenge and opportunity. I knew nothing about fish farming, but I discovered that despite the natural resources endowed on Ghana, there was a severe shortage of fish protein, a large proportion having to be imported to fill the gap. Right there I was confronted with the two ingredients that tickle my soul, and together with the odds of making it at fifty-fifty, it was a good enough risk for me to jump at the opportunity.

After five years of investment, which was not devoid of failures and mistakes, the business turned a corner and now provides employment to ten villagers. It is envisioned that within the next two years, Volta Tilapia Limited will be the major producer of fish in Ghana and abrogate the fish protein deficiency

Ghana faces. The company will also provide employment to many more people and probably serve as an educational center for prospective fish farmers.

The second emerging business is a hotel that will soon be commissioned in Accra. This is the first of many that I envisage will be the crown of my business career.

It will be an epitome of luxury unsurpassed by local competitors. This again is a feat that I challenged myself with, and it will be a disappointment if I do not achieve it.

I must not forget that being a doctor is a job, but running your own practice is a business. I have done this very well in Chicago; it is running with four providers. We provide concierge medical care to the elderly and bedridden in the comfort of their homes. We are doctors on wheels.

PHILANTHROPY

There is no joy to me if I am the only one who has and others do not have. I remind myself that if I had no one else to look after, I would by now have lots of money in my bank account. I do not have lots of money in my account because I use it to help people. I feel that I should always be the giver, and it feels strange to me when I receive a gift from someone. I am a philanthropist.

From the Philippines to Chicago and across Ghana, I have left my trail of charity work behind by touching the hearts and souls of people, making their lives better than what they were. The thanks of my beneficiaries, expressed and unexpressed, are the memories that nourish the heart of this philanthropist and are a blessing to my work. I am a proud receiver of such blessings and happy that people associate my name with philanthropy and not egocentricity.

My career in benevolence is just beginning, but I have many feathers in my cap already. In Chicago, I championed the cause to raise awareness of hepatitis. These are a group of viruses that lead to liver failure and death. I was a board member of the Georgia Doty Health Educational Fund in Chicago for many years. Through this organization, we set up many health fairs in communities in the South Side of Chicago. I gave multiple talks on various health issues, including hepatitis, to these communities in the bid to raise awareness and instill preventive behaviors. I was a guest on multiple television and radio programs featuring health issues in Chicago. Knowledge is power, and through these programs, I believe I empowered many people and changed their behaviors.

In the Philippines, I was an integral part of medical missions that provided needed help to remote villages. A country far from my homeland of Ghana, the Philippines is home to people who are similar and ever sincere and appreciative of the contributions I made to their lives.

In Ghana, I changed many lives through my benevolent work. Not only did I provide free medical care to people in various hospitals and clinics and on various organized health missions, but I also put strangers in private hospitals at cost to myself. These are people who were very sick and had no money for medical care that would have cost them their lives' savings. Their families usually could only look on helplessly as they perished.

Various orphanages have benefited from my generous donations over the years in the form of money and material, and my measure of achievement is when I see those orphans run to me anytime I visit.

In the medical block of Korle-Bu Teaching Hospital, which did not have an intensive care unit, I raised money from my classmates to purchase the needed equipment to set up a unit that would take care of the very sick.

BOARDROOM

Crowning all my achievements is the invitation to join the boardroom in Chicago. I was selected as a member of the board of directors for Michael Reese Hospital in Chicago in the early years of the new millennium. I felt this was a humbling honor bestowed on me by the chief executive officer of the hospital.

Looking back at the reason for my appointment, I did not think I was appointed by accident but rather as an independent judgment and prize for my efforts that I unconsciously offered to keep the hospital floating.

When I joined the hospital as a self-employed physician in 2001, it soon became apparent to those at the hospital that I was a businessman and a good doctor. Within six months of joining the hospital, I established a full medical practice and became the biggest admitter of patients. I approached the practice as a business, offering myself to the local community and educating its members through health fairs, radio, and television. The patients loved my touch and attention, and I soon became a household name. My practice grew so rapidly that even I was shocked.

My patients had the shortest hospital stays through my astute care. Recognizing that, the hospital board asked me to take care of patients who got admitted through the emergency room and had no means of paying for their care. My colleagues were not keen to care for them, and their prolonged stays in the hospital were making the hospital lose money. I willingly provided the care needed to them and saved the hospital a lot of money through diligent utilization of services.

I did this with a free spirit and did not ask for remuneration, and it paid off. I sat on the board of the hospital to steer it through its turbulent financial difficulties. This privileged position not only allowed me to offer my business expertise to a troubled hospital but also equipped me with the ability to manage my own business operations. Today, I am well equipped to analyze and sift through the chaff of any business opportunity presented to me, and I have the ability to figure out the odds of success and take the calculated risks.

FAMILY

By virtue of the financial support I provided, every member of my family has enjoyed free health care and free education. Coupled with the exodus from the village, they find themselves in the privileged middle class in Ghana. I have put their heads above water, and the rest is for them to swim to success.

Chapter 21

THE SCARY MOMENT

Many people have experienced events where they came to the crossroads of life and death. When you hear their stories, it means they survived the situation. The stories that are untold are the ones with the bad outcomes that, together with the victims, have disappeared into obscurity.

However scary and nerve-racking it may be for some people, I believe flying is the safest mode of transportation compared to vehicular. But when you embark on a journey in an airplane, "safest" does not mean a 100 percent guarantee. My scary moment came when something went wrong with what was a seemingly safe mode of transportation. It was frightening enough that, for the first time ever, I wished I had not immigrated to the United States to pursue my dreams.

I was flying from Minneapolis to Chicago sometime in 2012. It was going to be a one-hour trip in the summer. The skies were clear. The weather was good. The winds were still—a perfect summer day for outdoor activities.

I embarked on a journey from Los Angeles to Chicago with a change of flight in Minneapolis. The change of flight to Chicago was smooth, and the flight was on time. I had a perfect arrangement to land on time to attend my daughter's school play in which she was the lead actress. I had everything worked out, from the time the plane would land at Chicago O'Hare Airport to taxiing home, changing clothes, and driving to her school.

During the flight, I did not think anything was wrong. It was going well. When I looked at my watch, I noticed the flight was taking longer than anticipated. Soon after, the other passengers also began to express the same concern. Then, gradually, spreading like a wave, the concern engulfed the rest of the passengers when after two hours, we were still not landing.

Then an announcement came from the cockpit that we had been diverted back to Minneapolis to land because of a problem with the landing gear. The pilot, in a calm voice, explained that during the takeoff, one of the tires had blown up, and a mechanism to deploy one of the landing gears had become faulty. He reassured us that the engineer was working to fix the problem.

The looks on the faces of my fellow passengers said it all. Nerves were heightened. I immediately thought about the school play. The nervous passengers heckled the air stewards, who indeed were in the same bad situation as us. Their answers were vague but professional in an effort to allay anxiety in a bemoaning flock of worried passengers.

The second announcement from the cockpit came about fifteen minutes later. This was grim news and rather added salt to the wound. He announced that the engineer had been unsuccessful in his attempt to fix the problem. The airplane was going to land with two legs instead of three. He asked the air stewards to prepare us for a crash landing.

It was then that I thought I would never see my family again. The attempt to see the school play was a fiasco. Many thoughts went through my head. I had not yet accomplished what I had set out to do in this world. The self-blaming game came into play to determine whether the trip had been at all necessary to begin with.

The crew began to walk us through the posture to adapt during a crash landing. Emergency exit modality was rehearsed. Anyone wearing high-heeled shoes was advised to remove them. The cabin was immediately cleared of all obstructions. For the first time in many years, I listened verbatim to the detailed safety demonstration of the aircrew. It may well have been the last time I would have done that, and it was appropriate that I accorded them that respect.

As the flight was approaching the Minneapolis airport and we were able to discern the details on the ground, we noticed many emergency vehicles with their red and blue flashing lights dotted along the runway. That was the time it dawned that we were in real danger. At that point I wished I could just have jumped out through the window and parachuted to safety.

One could feel the absolute silence in the cabin as the flight attendants took their seats to prepare themselves for the ultimate ordeal. My adrenalin level heightened. My ears thumped with my heartbeat so loudly that I felt it echoed across the aisle. Amid the silence came the occasional heaving, retching, and vomiting of the distressed passengers.

As we approached closer, the pilot, as if chanting, repeated the SOS phrase "Mayday...Mayday...Mayday" several times. We heard the functioning landing gears deploy and the wings of the plane expand. Then the final word came to brace for landing.

We all exhibited our quickly learned posture. We saw the ground move fast underneath the plane as we bypassed some of the emergency vehicles. One set of landing gear touched the ground followed by the other. Then the plane tilted to one side, and the wing just touched the ground. Amid a loud screeching of the brakes and the final scraping of the one wing on the ground, the plane rapidly slowed until it came to a stop in the middle of the runway.

As we exhaled a sigh of relief that we were at last on the ground, the emergency vehicles rapidly approached the dysfunctional plane as if it were the beginning of the main danger. With express rapidity, we were immediately ordered to leave the plane to go onto a standby bus on the tarmac.

The drive to the terminal was very long. The joy on our faces showed it all. It was as if we were returning from a high school football match our team had won. The plane did not burst into flames as we had originally feared after landing. It was a happy ending to an adventurous trip to Los Angeles.

This experience reinforced my perception that when life's events, business proposals, and promises appear to coalesce into a successful outcome, it is prudent to wait for results before building castles.

It is never over until it is over, and it is always a good practice to prepare for the unexpected.

Chapter 22

MY TAKE ON LIFE

DO NOT BE YOUR OWN ENEMY

There are two parts of the mind. These are the positive and the negative. If you are presented with a situation or a problem, the positive part tells you all the reasons you can overcome it, and the negative part tells you all the reasons you cannot overcome it. The positive mind can also be characterized as the good mind that allows you the ability to make all the right choices, and the reverse is true for the negative mind. Usually the two minds exist in one person, but the preponderance of one or the other gives a person the trait of positive-mindedness or negative-mindedness. The positive-minded usually see the glass as half-full, and the negative-minded see the glass as half-empty. Of course, there are some people caught in the middle who are neither of the two, and they get carried between the two characteristics depending on the circumstances. A good balance is the ability to have a strong positive-minded tendency and consciously manage the negative mind.

When you allow the positive mind to be in charge when presented with a problem, the mind begins to wander in the land of possibilities, where solutions are packed together in a hierarchy. These solutions could be people, places, or ideas, but they all work together along the hierarchy to dissect and analyze the presented problem and, because it is a land of possibilities, offer a solution that is better than doing nothing. This could take days, months, or even years. It could be serendipity or destiny, each of which is good and could turn a problem into good fortune. Most people do not realize that this is what has happened to them, and when they begin to analyze their situations, they realize that had the problem not occurred, they would not be in the better position they find themselves in.

On the other hand, one can be presented with the same problem with the negative mind in charge. The land of negativity is presented to you. Here there is a pack of negatives in a hierarchy, which could be people, places, or ideas. Each of them has a good story of negative outcomes and gives you all the reasons on earth why this problem cannot be solved. Since the negative mind is more comfortable than a positive mind, the story is rationalized as such as it passes you down the ladder of the hierarchy. In the end, the problem is abandoned, and you find yourself in the same or a worse situation.

The ears represent funnels channeling ideas into the mind's positive and negative compartments. Positive input reinforces the positive mind, and likewise, negative input reinforces the negative mind. As these compartments get bombarded with information, the facts are analyzed and critiqued and then rationalized positively or negatively depending on which mind is in charge. Positive results will come from the positive mind with good reason, and negative results will come from the negative mind, all with very good reasons. When you surround yourself with positive-minded people, you will most likely get a better result than with negative-minded people.

While science is still struggling to find the physical structural defect in the brain to explain addiction, applying this phenomenon of positive and negative minds to addiction goes a long way to helping people. It forms the basis of psychotherapy and has been applied to help many addicts. We have known people who were addicted to food, drugs, alcohol, smoking, and so on and who one day just gave up the habit after being reminded of the harm. We call them strong-willed. I will call them strong positive-minded people. They came up with all the good reasons they should have their last joint, their last cigarette, and the last extra calories they do not need.

You will be your own enemy if you feed yourself with negative ideas. It takes you nowhere. It will sink you. Always surround yourself with good people who are willing to contribute positives.

PURSUIT OF DREAMS

Everyone should have a dream of how they want their world to be in the future. This is a great gift that every human is endowed with. Some people have small dreams, and others have big dreams. However big or small our dreams are, they form the basis of our zeal to progress as humans. It is the blueprint with which we navigate this world in search of a better life. It is a continuum of aspiration passed on from generation to generation. It is what shapes a family to be rich or poor. It is the dream that shapes a people and makes a nation great or weak. It is the dream that has made our world become better and better.

The dream starts with the parent who already has an idea of what the child's world should be in the future. Usually it is a dream world that they could not achieve. They initiate the dream process by a means available to them, usually education. The child, gaining cognizance of his or her world, takes over the baton of the dream and refashions, refines, and repackages it to be his or her own. The process continues when this child becomes a parent.

We must dream as big and as much as we can, and we should not stop dreaming. When dreams stop, we do not progress. Big dreams are good, but do not build castles in the sky. We should be mindful that the dreams must be realistic.

Unrealistic dreams may never be achieved and may lead to great disappointment in the world of the negative-minded personalities. But we should not be fooled by this broad generalization because positive personalities have turned unrealistic dreams into discoveries. Who would have thought in the years before Christ that landing on the moon one day was a possibility? The dreamer would have been jeered and mocked and even jailed for voicing a dream like that.

Dreams should be fashioned along the sit-crawl-walk-and-run principle. So you could have a big dream that you may never achieve in your lifetime, but you also have a multitude of smaller dreams on the path to get to the big one. So you aim at landing on the sun, and when you fail to do so, you land on Mars. This is perfectly acceptable.

Arrange your dreams in a timed, stepwise fashion. The smaller dreams are taken care of first in a specified time period, keeping in mind that it is just a stage for the process of the big dream and is a means to an end. It is therefore perfectly acceptable to be cleaning someone's floor for a dollar if this process is considered just a stage.

At any stage of the dreaming process, enjoy it, and apply all your human effort to perform it with your utmost ability. Be it a trade, an education, or an apprenticeship, applying your best prepares you for the next stage. In addition, be aware that there is always an audience acknowledging your effort, and one of them could be a bouncing pad for the next stage of the dream process.

Never dream small; always dream big. After all, it costs nothing to dream it. But be realistic when you dream it, and take baby steps before you run.

THOUGHT BROADCASTING

It is bad enough to have the illusion of someone else broadcasting your thoughts. This is a mental illness categorized as schizophrenia. But what is worse is when you are broadcasting your own uncensored thoughts to others. This could be too much for the interlocutor and earn you a name as a bragger or talker.

Your ideas and thoughts are bona fide personal property. You own them. Keep them held tight, and do not divulge them anytime one comes into your head. What comes out must be time and place appropriate and measured. Otherwise, you will quickly be associated with the derogatory labels of "bragger" and "talker," expressed or unexpressed by your interlocutors.

If you have an exciting big dream that you want to pursue, do not quickly announce it. Since it is a dream, it may not come to pass, and if you do discuss it, you will raise expectations in your audience. You have also set up unnecessary pressure on yourself to make sure the dream is achieved. If the dream is achievable, the pressure may be good fuel to propel you to success. If it is not achievable, you may either let it go and risk the chance of getting labeled a bragger or be forced into doing the wrong things to please your audience. More importantly, your dream may be stolen away.

What if you say nothing until the dream is almost in sight? You have no pressure to either please anyone or even achieve the dream. All you will have in this situation is admiration and a bravo.

When presented with a business opportunity, the first thing is to keep quiet. Do not announce it. Let the opportunity sink in, and allow yourself time to ponder over it. If it is too good to be true, perhaps it is, and time will tell you. Perform a litmus test with experts in the area of the business to get an initial reaction. Then select the audience you know will help advance the business opportunity. If the opportunity fails, the selected few will understand and need no explanation. However, if everyone else knows about the opportunity and it fails, you have some explaining to do before you are labeled a talker.

What if you are a politician? Thought broadcasting is a perfect tool. The purpose is different. Backing this skill with charisma and astuteness will land you a perfect job.

BE YOURSELF AND NOT SOMEONE ELSE

At some stage in life, we all dreamed of who, where, and what we wanted to be. This is perfectly normal and serves as a driving force, like a decoy in the Olympic long-distance race. When growing up, we are encouraged to identify people as role models in our lives, and not infrequently, we are well served by doing so. It is not uncommon to see families with generations of lawyers, doctors, and politicians.

But desiring to be someone else is a little too much and would signal lack of self-worth. It can lead you into trouble. Let's say you want to be someone rich and famous. You must realize that most people are born with nothing. This person has gone through a process to achieve goals to the point of recognition. You are completely oblivious to this process. Digging into the process would reveal the toil that allowed this to happen. When this is made apparent to you, you begin to realize how ridiculous the idea was.

I have read the story of a young man who wanted to be rich and famous. His process was to see a powerful medicine man. He was told that this was possible, but he would have to sacrifice his dad. He was given a poison to put into his dad's food. His dad found out after taking a bite that there was poison in his food. The young man confessed and got arrested. Stories like this are very common in many parts of the world.

Avoiding being subservient to someone else prepares you to be yourself with confidence. Do not let people walk all over you, and always stand your ground, but be polished about it. Saying yes to someone rich and famous before he or she completes his or her sentence can be construed as weakness and must be avoided. Remember not to worship any human being. Be honored when you meet a rich and famous person, but never melt down with goose pimples. Walk with your chest out, and be confident that you are you.

BE SELFLESS-HEAVEN IS EARTH

Many of us are always brought up with the notion that when you do good things, you will go to heaven, and when you do bad things, you will go to hell. This is fair, especially when you believe in life after death. Religious people are guided by this, and all we think of is how sweet it will be to find ourselves in heaven. Nobody has come back to tell us how nice heaven is or how bad hell is.

I have never seen any concept of hell before. But our imagination takes us into the world of Satan. There we believe it is packed with all the bad people you can imagine, including murderers, armed robbers, fornicators, and the like. They are probably in an inferno, gnashing their teeth in perpetual suffering. And Satan and his disciples are jeering and cheering, giving one another high fives for their feats in drawing the hard-core people of humanity into their camp.

I certainly saw a movie of the concept of heaven, which makes you feel like you should die immediately and join the perpetual enjoyment. I saw the angels with big wings all in white, the good people all dressed in white, live bands playing the finest music the world has ever created, and an atmosphere of perpetual happiness. There was an image of God smiling and continually blessing everybody.

These descriptions are all imaginative and probably a mirage. I have personally experienced the concept of heaven on earth, and I believe others unknowingly have too.

We commonly hear people making reference to karma. This is defined in Hinduism and Buddhism as the force generated by a person's actions to influence transmigration and, in its ethical consequences, determine the nature of the person's next existence. But it is literally used to imply the reward, whether good or bad, for one's actions. What we are saying is that people have already presumed a bad outcome for someone's life because of the bad things he or she did to someone else in the recent past. Since hell is a concept, I would picture this as real hell, tangible hell.

By the same token, have you realized that some wealthy people are more generous than the less wealthy? By wealthy, I do not mean people who have millions of dollars but rather those who have more relative wealth than their neighbors. Have you thought of the fact that they are generous because they are wealthy, or are they wealthy because they are generous? It is like the question of what came first, the chicken or the egg. Since I cannot speak for others, I will speak for myself to prove that the egg came before the chicken. With all the good things happening to me now in business, I am no doubt basking in heaven. I am not rich, but I am blessed.

Being good to a neighbor, stranger, workmate, boss, or anybody pays off only if the intent is solely for that purpose and without any ulterior motives. Never sell your body or part of your body to achieve this goodness. Never consciously expect a reward from the good things you have done for somebody. Allow the heavens to be your witness and pay you back.

As you continue to be selfless, you progressively find yourself surrounded by people with good vibes. Consider this a stage where you are performing a show. If the show is nice, you get a cheer from the audience. As you expand your audience base, the more popular you become. The audience begins to make associations with your name. Suddenly the audience begins to think about you when you are not even thinking about them. When you get to this level, you have arrived at the doors of heaven. Its doors begin to open for you even when you are not expecting it. Challenges begin to be easier to overcome. Living begins to be effortless. You know who to call for help, and you know they will never fail you. Think about this when you get contacted for jobs and business opportunities. They do not come out of the blue. Somebody whom you touched one day has remembered you and said that this opportunity would best suit you. Let this sink in that your previous kind gesture is paying off.

Think about enjoying the heaven here first, and it will prepare you to enjoy the imaged one even better when you pass on.

I have known people who claim they love God a lot. They go to church frequently, they pray every day, and so on. Yet they do all the wrong things to their neighbors. The neighbor whom you can see with your own eyes, you hate, yet God, who you cannot see, you claim you love so much. This boggles my mind, and I do not know the word to describe this dichotomy. Does "hypocrisy" make sense?

FOLLOWERS AND LEADERS

These human characteristics are inherent traits you are born with. You are either a leader or a follower. Leaders characteristically become business owners, politicians, presidents, chief executive officers, and so on. Followers take instructions. Each of these characteristics has unique features. But while I am painting in broad strokes about each one of them, I am mindful that there are overlaps.

Leaders are usually global thinkers; they think outside the box and are by no means narrow-minded people. They are risk-takers and are not afraid to fail. They have poor attention to detail. They have the power to control other people's actions. They think before they talk. They have the ability to multiply themselves by delegating. They do not beat around the bush.

Followers are usually skilled with attention to detail, are good at executing given tasks, are extremely pleasant, and are ready to please others. They are hesitant to take risks. They drag their feet.

What is really important is to identify where you belong and pursue it. Success depends on how good you perform your role as a follower or a leader and not whether you are a leader or a follower. In human society, we cannot all be leaders or followers, but we should try to be good leaders and good followers. Failure comes when you are trying to be who you are not.

Leaders finding themselves in an employed situation are usually unhappy with their jobs, but more importantly, they will do or have done something about it. They probably will not stay for too long and, because they are risk-takers, move on to the next opportunity until they reach their level.

Put followers in that same situation. Even though they are not happy, they are afraid to take the plunge and are content to kick the can down the road. They are admirable and successful when they identify themselves as such and are awarded the highest level of appreciation.

MIND YOUR OWN BUSINESS

The first day I took my daughter to her middle school, the principal showed us around. While we were on the tour, he introduced us to their school code, called the Eagle's Way. When I pressed him for an explanation, he said, "Do not touch anything, and do not let anything touch you." He further specified that the children should keep their arms, fingers, and bodies to themselves. By so doing, they would not be fighting with one another, the library books would be kept intact on the shelves where they were supposed to be, and so on. I believe the principle worked, and that was why he sold it to every child who came through the door.

A dormant brain and dormant time are two very important assets one can have. However, when you are endowed with these two assets, they can be turned into either a weapon of mass destruction or a weapon of mass construction.

The astute and progressive will rapidly turn the latter asset into very productive outcomes involving business, education, sports, and so on. These people take so much advantage of this asset that they quickly run out of it. Then they have no room to do anything else and lament that there is not enough time in the world.

The other group of people will use this asset as a weapon of mass destruction. They cannot help themselves. They quickly become magnets of gossip. Since bad news sells better than no news, they quickly find the market for it. They attract like minds to form a team. The conversations always end up about someone else in a derogatory fashion. They have too much time on their hands and meddle in other people's business.

People who break the code of the Eagle's Way generally have certain characteristics. Filling your time and head with other people's business and gossip deprives you of the bandwidth to do anything progressive for yourself. When the progressives are using this time profitably and complaining that they do not have enough of it, the gossipers are using their valuable time and energy to listen to, analyze, gossip about, and destroy someone else.

It does not take a rocket scientist to analyze the trajectory of the two groups of people. Unless you win the lottery, productivity and success are time dependent, and if the two groups of people are in a race to an end, the one that puts in the utmost effort will certainly be the champion. Moreover, since the mind has two parts, positive and negative, with the ears being large funnels, negativity feeds the negative mind, and the outcome is always negative.

The resultant unproductive anarchy creates chaos in the immediate environment and, be it in the home or with friends, can lead to unnecessary altercations and fighting. Small minds allow this to happen to them, and certainly filling their minds with other people's stuff does not allow them any room to be productive for their own benefit. They always reach the finish line late.

BE A LISTENER, NOT A TALKER

Many people have had interactions with another person who talked a lot. At the end of the encounter, you felt your eardrum had been so badly bombarded that a recovery was much needed.

Talking is a human gift to communicate ideas and feelings to another person. It is a useful tool, without which mankind would not have had dominion over other primates. It is important also to remember that it is a two-way street with an interlocutor who must be given a chance.

Allow talkers the room to talk, and they will fill you up with stuff that you do not even want to know about them. Sometimes this transforms into bragging, at which point a line is drawn between a talker and a braggart.

In business, talkers have a great asset when they use their prowess to make you buy things you do not intend to. They are great salespeople.

Listeners are like sponges that take it all in. They assimilate information, analyze it, and spit out wisdom. Spend the same time with a talker and a listener, and you will feel you have spent more relative time with the listener than the talker. Even though the two assets may be good in many ways, one would gravitate to a listener rather than a talker. Doors open more for listeners than talkers.

WHO DO I WANT TO BE?

I want to be myself. But I have admiration for great people in recent memory, the likes of which include Mahatma Gandhi, Martin Luther King Jr., and Nelson Mandela. The commonality they shared was love of people and creating equality among them, and they went the extra mile. I share the same values, and I would not have acted differently had I been in their shoes.

Chapter 23

PEOPLE WHO HAVE IMPACTED MY LIFE

MY PARENTS: THE RATE-DETERMINING STEP

I t goes without saying that your parents should be the first influences on your life; after all, they brought you into this world. Sometimes it does not happen the way it should, and rather, they turn their backs on their struggling progeny. But the attribute I accord to my parents is that they did not only meet expectations but went above and beyond their abilities and put me in the special place that made my progression to success more easily attainable.

That special place was my secondary school. It was that simple, but it was an important crossroad and rate-determining step in my life. At the time I was of age to attend a secondary school, my parents were at their wits' end financially. Money was tight. They had no reserves for their retirement. Most of my contemporaries were in the same boat as me. Their parents gave up. They ended up on the farms and plantations to do manual labor after graduating from middle school at sixteen years old. Most of them remained in the village and, obeying the prevailing statistics of life expectancy of fifty-five to sixty-five years, have passed on into the next world, some before even meeting the village statistics.

When my parents discovered my potential, they scrambled their resources to invest in me. I could see the drain and strain when I was about to go to school and they had to give me that money for the school's fees. When I received the money and it was in all denominations, I knew the vault was completely emptied. They were down to their last savings.

All I needed to do was not fail them. But first I had to not fail myself. And from the age of fifteen, I have been equipped with a double-edged sword to fight failure. I still have the sword, which is getting sharper and sharper as I climb to the apogee of life's success.

BIG J, GHANA: BUSINESS OF MEDICINE

Big J was a very successful young doctor when I was in medical school. He had self-made wealth through hard work. He was the first among his year group to start a clinic while he was an intern and the first to buy a car. His private patient base grew rapidly not only because he was a good doctor but also because he was a nice doctor. He came into the limelight when his private patient base, even as an intern, surpassed the most experienced professors who were still training him.

Intuitively, I found a similarity between him and me. In the fourth year of medical school, I became friends with him. I wanted to learn how he was so good at setting up a clinic so quickly and successfully, even as an intern. I followed him to his clinics and witnessed his interactions with his patients. I soon discovered that he did not practice medicine as a doctor but practiced the profession as a business with customer satisfaction being the central theme. He did not wear the ego of a doctor who kept patients at arm's distance but rather made the patient feel he was on their side. He saw every patient as a customer who must be satisfied at every visit. He treated patients with great respect and at their levels. Every patient walked out of his consulting room with all their concerns satisfactorily addressed. In a country where doctors were prohibited from advertising themselves in the media and on billboards, word of mouth was the best form of advertisement, and his satisfied patients passed the word around.

I got it. I made use of this in my own medical practice in the United States, and it worked. In private practice, considering medicine as a business allows you to apply all the rules of any business entity to make it successful. Patient satisfaction always translates into wealth.

DR. JOHN APPIAH: COMPASSION

Dr. Appiah is a successful medical practitioner in private practice in Koforidua, located in the eastern region of Ghana. His first posting after graduating from Ghana Medical School was at St. Joseph Hospital in Koforidua. This hospital is located within the vicinity of Pope John Secondary School, where I started my secondary education.

I first met Dr. Appiah when I was an inpatient at St. Joseph Hospital. I was fifteen years old then. I was blown away by the way he talked to me and the care he gave me. That was the first and last time I was an inpatient, and looking back, I still feel his healing touch. When I was discharged from the hospital, I immediately decided I was going to be just like him.

I reconnected with him many years after, when I became a medical student. He became my mentor. During the holidays, he provided me a place to stay in his house and fed me so that I could have the opportunity to be with him during his consultations and his inpatient rounds. I learned his skills of talking to patients and the gentle touch he used in his examinations.

Dr. Appiah went even further to financially support me during the hard times in medical school. I was able to buy new clothes with his support to look decent among my mates in school. I remember that in those days any extra money I received from someone was like gold, and I made use of it judiciously. This is how I feel today about the financial support Dr. Appiah afforded me at the time.

I entrusted my dad into his hands, and he became his doctor until my dad passed away. As money was tight in my family at the time, Dr. Appiah, with his kind heart, gracefully provided a free service to my dad.

Dr. John Appiah served as a very important component of the jigsaw puzzle that delivered me into prosperity, and I am very grateful.

FATHER SAMUEL BATSA, GHANA: "REMEMBER WHERE YOU COME FROM"

Father Batsa is now a retired Roman Catholic priest residing in Ghana. He was the first Krobo priest from our community. Soon after his ordination, he was posted to our diocese. For the first time in the history of our community, Mass was served and preached in our local language. As a result, he won admiration from the young and old alike. His name became iconic. He was revered and quickly became a role model in our community. One of his admirers was, of course, my dad. It was because of this that my dad wanted me to become a Catholic priest.

Father Batsa also doubled as a tutor in English literature at Pope John Secondary School and a housemaster responsible for the well-being of one of the dormitories. During my secondary school education, Father Batsa was at one time or another either my literature master or my housemaster. Since he was my father's idol, it felt as if he were an extension of my father during my sojourn at the boarding school. And indeed, it literally was.

One time I was mixed up with the kids of the rich families and copying their truancy. These kids always disobeyed the rules of the school and were frequently in trouble with the school authorities. I tried disobeying the rules one time by ignoring the curfew for bedtime. I stayed up late to study, and he caught me. Like my father would have done, Father Batsa gave me a talk and meted me the appropriate punishment.

This derailed any ambition I had to follow the bad behavior of the "cool" guys in the school and reminded me that I did not belong to the group of privileged kids, and if I wanted to become like them, I had to work a bit harder. It was a life-changing event for me, swaying me away from a path of doom to that of success.

DR. GORDON THOMAS, UNITED KINGDOM: PROFESSIONAL INTEGRITY

Dr. Thomas is a great Welshman from South Wales in the United Kingdom. He is also a renowned physician specializing in pulmonary medicine, which studies diseases of the lungs. He practiced his specialty exclusively in his home region, Wales, at Nevill Hall Hospital in Abergavenny.

Wales was once the nerve center of the coal mining industry in Great Britain. However, the adverse environmental impact of coal has caused this industry to collapse in recent years while clean energy has taken over as the new cool trend. This industrial prowess was accompanied by unforeseen consequences of severe lung disease called pneumoconiosis. In addition, smoking was rampant in the coal miners, and that led to additional lung disease processes called chronic obstructive pulmonary disease and lung cancer. It was also the era of reawakening when bad asbestos was discovered to cause multiple lung cancers.

Dr. Thomas was revered as a consultant treating these complicated lung diseases and training young doctors. Even though he was a great and experienced physician, he was not the favorite of the medical staff. This was because of his code of textbook medical practice and attention to detail.

It was against this backdrop that Dr. Thomas hired me as doctor-in-training in the position of a senior house officer to learn pulmonary medicine. This allowed me to take charge of all the complicated lung diseases one can imagine.

Under his strict guidance, I navigated through the nuances of pulmonary medicine for three years and became an expert. I have carried over his attention to detail for the rest of my medical career, and today I live with that principle of detailed medicine practice.

Again, in medical practice as in business, you interact with people with all kinds of frustrations and mannerisms. These are sometimes projected onto the treating doctor with inappropriate expressions, intentionally or unintentionally. The natural reflex is to respond in the manner in which one is assaulted. The cultured doctor remains calm and lets silence defuse the situation. Dr. Thomas inculcated in me these qualities that shame the assailants for their approach.

Dr. Thomas and I became very close friends outside of medicine. He was instrumental in the visa appeal process when my critically ill mother was declined a visa to come for a medical treatment in the United Kingdom.

I think of Dr. Thomas today as the man who taught me medicine.

DR. ENRIQUE BECKMAN, USA: CORPORATE AMERICA'S BOARDROOM

I once encountered an old lady on an airplane with a magazine in her hands. There was nothing strange about this at all. After all, it was a long flight, and boredom is certainly a force to reckon with, especially if you are unable to take advantage of all the in-flight entertainment. Upon looking closely, I noticed the magazine was turned upside down, but it was obvious that her gaze was fixated on the page. It was none of my business since I always obeyed the Eagle's Way code. But my curiosity was certainly aroused. Just before the flight landed, she asked me to help her complete the landing card. It was then that I realized she was a complete illiterate, spoke only a local Ghanaian dialect, and was excited to visit her grandchildren in London.

For a successful businessman who has never been to a business school, reading the financial report of your company and being able to make sense out of it and use it for future projections and forecasts can be daunting. Just like the grandma described above, you could find yourself wallowing from page to page, unable to distinguish the head or tail of the report.

This was how it felt when I was first invited to be a member of the board of directors for Michael Reese Hospital. After multiple board meetings to steer the hospital out of deep waters, and with personal effort, I became conversant with financial reports and able to make deductions and manipulations in any way I wanted.

Dr. Enrique Beckman was the chief executive officer of the hospital at the time. He was a pathologist and a successful businessman who grew his pathology practice into a huge business empire serving multiple hospitals in the Chicago area. Being a successful businessman, he was the obvious choice for the CEO of the hospital. Since like attracts like, we soon became friends. When he got to know me better, he gave me the opportunity to serve on the board.

This was a singular opportunity given to me to enrich my knowledge on how to run a successful business. The experience is guiding me as I build my own business empire. One day when I am not reading the report of my business empire upside down, I will remember Dr. Enrique Beckman.

DR. AYISI KWADWO, GHANA: A RELIABLE BROTHER

Like many people, I have made many friends during my life's journey. And for a variety of reasons, these friends move on. You later catch up with them. But sometimes distances become a silent enemy that gradually gnaws away at the good memories.

However, some of your friends never leave your life, and eventually it becomes an embarrassment to introduce them as friends because they are best described as brothers or sisters.

This is what happened to Dr. Ayisi, who is nicknamed Sharon. We are good friends, but it's best to say we are brothers. We first met at Pope John Secondary. His background mirrored mine like a rose that blossomed in the desert. We both became doctors despite the odds against us. We both used the rule of sit, crawl, walk, and run to make it into prosperity. His prosperity stemmed from beating the drums in Ghana and mine from hustling abroad.

Our roads crossed when I opened my options for opportune moments in business investment in Ghana. I have relied on him 100 percent for openings, and he has never failed me. Even though I am not always in Ghana, I have relied on him to make the right decisions for me, and he has selflessly done so and beyond. Today, I owe the success of the hotel under construction to his stalwart support, without which it would have been an impossible dream.

For my family to thrive in Ghana and be successful, I have committed myself to providing them with free education and free health care at my expense. Sharon, having his own private hospital in Ghana, has made it possible for my family to receive good health care at my expense but at a fraction of the cost. I owe my mother's longevity to the very good care she received from Sharon.

Many doctors of my generation always carry guilt about leaving the country to serve other nations. We were beneficiaries of free medical education in Ghana. I share that guilt. I wanted to repay Mother Ghana for affording me medical knowledge free of charge. Sharon made this possible. He opened up business opportunities for me, and through investments I have been able to repay Mother Ghana many times over.

MS. AGATHA AWAH, GHANA: A RESPONSIBLE SIBLING

It is not uncommon for siblings to be the worst business partners. Some people even have a mantra that business is best done with strangers rather than family. The complacency regarding responsibility toward a sibling's property can sometimes be taken so far that when a business is entrusted to a family member, it often leads to ruin and catastrophe.

It is against this backdrop that I regard my sister Agatha as a needle in the haystack. She is one of a pair of twins and the eldest of my mother's progeny. She is much older than me and left home before I was born. Today, I revere her as a parent rather than a sister.

She retired from the Ghana military, where she served for many years as an officer in the signal regiment. Since then she has been involved in various business activities, including import and export and poultry farming. When I discovered the huge deficiency of fish protein in Ghana, I discussed with her if she could take on fish farming. I knew it was unfair for me to ask her to partake in my risky venture for many reasons. The first reason was that we both had no clue about fish farming, and the odds against the venture were very high. The second reason was that she had to relocate from the comfort of big-city life in Accra and settle in a remote village located near the Volta Lake. The third reason was that she entrusted her life to a risk-taker and was willing to do so without getting paid.

Without hesitation, she jumped on the risky boat ride with me for the adventure of fish farming. With her at the helm and me blindfolded, I aided her to navigate through the process of the fish farming business.

We acquired a piece of snake-infested land in the middle of nowhere near the Volta Lake. Since funds were tight, she sacrificed her comfort for the growth of the business. She relocated there into a very basic housing unit. She had no vehicle, and the only means of transport was walking or being a passenger on a motorcycle. She has inherent self-motivating ability and huge business acumen. She judiciously used my little financial investments and grew the business.

In the village, she met many failed start-up fish farmers from whom she acquired valuable knowledge. This indispensable knowledge was used to structure our emerging business. She educated herself on fish farming practices at a course run by the Water Research Institute in Akosombo. She hired an expert from the institute as a consultant for our venture.

I underestimated the likelihood of a seventy-year-old retired military officer turning my dream of a fish farm into a reality within five years. Today,

Volta Tilapia Limited has provided employment for ten permanent workers and another ten casual laborers during harvesting. The farm is on track to become one of the top three tilapia farms in Ghana in the next two years.

This achievement would not have been possible but for the selfless dedication to hard work, astute business ability, honesty, and military discipline of my sister Agatha. Together we have provided employment to the youth in the small village and helped Mother Ghana be self-sufficient in fish protein.

MR. MORGAN CARTER, USA (DECEASED): PUBLICITY

Mr. Carter was a renowned radio and television host based in Chicago. He was very charismatic with great oratory ability. His show was appropriately dubbed the "world conversation starter," which many households across Chicago watched on cable television. He was a visionary during the early days of the Internet and was one of the pioneers who made use of the World Wide Web to broaden his audience. He was very influential in the media council of Chicago and brought many individuals, businesses, and politicians into the limelight.

Little did I know who he was. I was introduced to him after my board meeting for a charitable organization. He had been limping for the previous six months in an orthopedic shoe, and my curiosity was focused on his foot. It came to light that despite all his great work, he was a noncompliant diabetic who had developed bone infections in his foot. The foot was so swollen that he had not been able to wear shoes for over six months.

I offered to treat him at no charge in my clinic as he was one of many Americans who had not bothered to buy any medical insurance. Within three months, his foot was completely healed, and he was back in his shoes.

We became friends immediately. As our friendship grew, he gradually revealed to me the nature of his work. It became clear that he wanted to educate his audience on medical issues afflicting the population, like obesity and diabetes, of which he was a victim. He created a sideshow on his platform for me and named it *Doctor in the House*, for which I was the cohost. This was the legacy Mr. Carter gave me, a defining moment in my medical career and business in Chicago that projected me into the limelight in Chicago households.

I was exposed to television and radio for the first time. I used the opportunity to raise awareness about many disease processes, like the obesity epidemic that is afflicting many of my patients in Chicago. The unintended consequence was that I became a household name to his audience, and this allowed my medical business in Chicago to flourish. I was featured in the *Chicago Tribune* as the doctor who had brought life to the impoverished and medically underserved South Side of Chicago.

Mr. Carter passed away a few years later after a massive heart attack. I cherish his soul and the door he opened for me.

MS. DEANA SAMMONS: VALUE FOR MONEY

Deana is a pretty, naturally blond woman whom I met at the beginning of my business career in Chicago. The chief operating officer of Michael Reese Hospital introduced her to me. It was at the time when the hospital had discovered my true potential for making a major contribution to its success. They wanted to help my young medical business flourish, which in turn would benefit the hospital tremendously.

Deana at the time was well adept with the medical business in Chicago. She was co-owner of an ambulance company and a nursing home. As a result, she knew the administrative staffs of most of the nursing homes in Chicago. She was astute in business and used the principle of sit, crawl, walk, and run to make it to the top. She came from a wealthy family, but unlike her siblings, who took to the family business of construction, she used her naturally inherent ability to set up her own business empire and became successful.

She is also naturally benevolent and has touched many unfortunate souls in the South Side of Chicago. Almost every weekend, she was involved in providing food to and finding shelter for the homeless in the impoverished part of Chicago.

As soon as I met her, I immediately knew we were similar. She was no doubt a born businesswoman. She was always thinking outside the box and was fearless in making bold business decisions. She wore many hats skillfully and was in many places at the same time.

Putting us together was probably one of the best decisions the hospital administration ever made. Within six months, Deana helped me to be on staff in most of the nursing homes in the vicinity of the hospital. With her influence, coupled with my personal hard work, I became busy very quickly. This translated into multiple admissions to the hospital, which earned me huge recognition.

As I got to know Deana, she instilled good business practices in me. She possessed the typical measured enthusiasm of a true businesswoman. Money does not come easily, and what sounds too good to be true probably is. She would not be carried away with promises of a new business proposal until after her critical analysis. She would not broadcast her ideas of a new business until the business took shape, a good practice that put her into the category of a doer and not a talker. She inculcated in me that I do not have a second chance to make a first impression, and I have benefited from this ideology in my business career.

The most defining moment of a true friendship was when Deana lifted me when I was at my lowest ebb. For risk-takers in business, things do not always go the way they are intended to. It was one of those moments in 2008 in Chicago when I was a victim of one of my big dreams. The United States' economy went into a deep recession, and with it I went. It was at the point that I could not even afford a car to use for work. When I looked around, the only one I could call on was Deana. Deana made a phone call to a car dealership, and within six hours, I drove away with a brand-new BMW 5 Series.

Deana steadily built her business empire, exceeding all the milestones she set for herself, and is now selflessly serving humanity through her charity work in Pakistan with her husband, helping poor children have a good education and health care.

MRS. MICHELE AWAH: L'AIDE DE CAMP

During times of war, many challenges come one's way. Strategists present a multifaceted front to the enemy to pose a challenge to them. And winning could be dependent on these little changes.

My biggest-ever war was the divorce proceeding between Linda and me. Even though she filed for the breakup, I was responsible for paying her legal fees and mine. She was unwilling and uncompromising on every issue and was set to drag the matter out in court for as long as it would take to get what she wanted. The combined legal fees for which I was responsible were well over $100,000 and rising.

This was the time Michele came into my life, and it appeared we were going to get married. One time after court, she dragged Linda aside and explained to her how stupid it was to put these huge sums of money into the pockets of lawyers. When Linda came to that realization, she backed down and became more reasonable. I have no idea what the final bill would have been without Michele's intervention.

To grow any business, you need a reliable personnel force, one that is selfless and committed to carrying out the agenda set for the company. This inherent force has allowed companies to blossom. For those who have never owned a business before, it sounds easy to find the right personnel, but I am preaching to the choir for the experienced businessperson. I have been a victim of false personnel, some of whom included very close family members, and I had no hesitation in firing personnel who did not meet my expectations.

When I allowed Michele to be the director of my infant medical practice, I immediately discovered a potential force on the horizon. She put all her effort into understanding the nuances of running a medical practice. When she got it, she dedicated herself to the business as if it were her own and adorned it with her mind and soul. Tirelessly and selflessly, she gave the business a thrust that has exponentially projected it into the stratosphere within a short period of time.

She is the proud face of my burgeoning new-age medical practice, and her selfless stewardship has chalked up many significant milestones in its success. This will allow me to showcase my new model of profitable medical practice in a world where traditional medical practices are now seeing diminishing returns because of reduced reimbursement and rising overhead costs.

To give Caesar what he is due, Michele is hands-down and not hands-up. My past experience always put me on high alert for takers. Michele is not one.

MERCY AMIHERA: NOT JUST A DOMESTIC

When my wife, Michele, had a child, Ama, she was also deeply involved in my rapidly growing medical practice as the manager. Even though she was working from home, the two jobs became very daunting for her. She got to the point where it was almost impossible to perform the motherhood job and continue the medical business career efficiently.

Having recognized this predicament, we decided to seek the help of a domestic worker. The ethnic choice was biased toward Ghanaian origin so as to augment and induce a bit of the African culture into my little girl. I made one phone call to the Ghanaian community, and within one day, Mercy was presented to us as the first candidate for an interview. It was love at first sight when my wife met Mercy. She was hired on the spot as she carried the air of motherly serenity.

Mercy is originally from Ghana, is about my age, and immigrated to the United States as an adult. We are culturally similar as she has not shied away from all the culinary delicacies from Ghana. Hence, she doubled as a cook and also a caretaker for my little girl Ama.

Her qualities gave a tremendous amount of relief to my wife, who is now able to devote quality time to the medical practice. We are able to have quality African food in the home. The frequent aromas emanating from our home from her African cooking will get any passerby's mouth watering with anticipation of having a Ghanaian cuisine experience. Her killer foods include corned beef stew, bean stew, and Jollof rice. Yummy!

Mercy introduced us to her family, who still reside in Ghana. Her brother, Albert, and I have become friends because of our commonality in business. As time went on, my and Michele's initial employer-employee relationship with Mercy grew into an African extended family system to the point that today we no longer consider her a domestic but one of the family. I now see Mercy as a sister, and Michele has been deeply involved in Mercy's well-being and the care of her children and grandchildren.

In times of turbulence in my home, as does happen between couples on occasion, Mercy always reminds me to look forward, concentrate, and finish the hotel. I have repeated to myself, "Look forward, concentrate, and finish the hotel," so many times that it has become like a song in my head. I have applied these words in my head in many instances when I became frustrated. Mercy has recognized that this is my life goal and it would just be a dream if I allowed bumps in the road to hinder its completion. I owe Mercy respect for her encouragement.

I have tremendous respect for the power of other people in one's life journey. The choice of selecting persons into your life circle can make or unmake you. The old adage that states, "Show me your friend, and I will show you your character," always stands to be true.

Successful persons can always look back and name the people who made it possible for them. In my experience, these persons must not be just rich or poor; they must just be good people.

Ensuring good people around you in any business venture will almost always contribute to your success.

Chapter 24

THE BIG BANG

I have successfully achieved my educational goal. My business career is comfortably on autopilot in a positive trajectory as I am discovering new frontiers. And now I am on my third career goal of giving back to humanity. So far I have only scratched the surface of benevolence. I am now ready to take it to the next level. It must therefore be by design that I was introduced to Vincent Woode. His story is what I call the big bang.

A few months ago, I visited Ghana on a business trip. Near the end of my trip, I attended an activity of my alma mater's Pope John Old Boy Association. During this process, I ran into an acquaintance from Metro TV, a news anchor named Harriet Nartey. She told me about a fund-raiser to save the life of a young man with brain tumor that was going badly. I asked her to send me the fund-raising video. A few days after I arrived in the United States, I received the video, in which a young man was helplessly seeking funding to have surgery to remove his brain tumor so he could live. I watched the video over and over again.

While I was watching the video, I thought of the pain and suffering of a young man whose plight, if he were living in the United States, would have been considered lower in hierarchy than that of a cat or a dog from the way his countrymen had left him to perish from a treatable and potentially curable disease. What was between him and death was about $20,000, which was nothing for a few rich folks like footballers, politicians, businessmen, and pastors, each of whom, chipping in a tiny fraction of their wealth, could save a life. Cats and dogs in advanced countries would not be left untreated for so long with a brain tumor of this nature. I would not personally have allowed any of my family members to live with a brain tumor for four years like Vincent did.

I was so touched by the impending doom that no sooner had I completed watching the video than I reached out to Harriet for Vincent's telephone number. I immediately called Vincent and introduced myself. I told him I wanted to help him find the money. Even though it was a telephone conversation, I could feel Vincent through his voice. The shudder in his voice during the brief conversation felt like I had touched the core of his soul.

From this point onward, even though I had not met Vincent before, he and I became close friends. Each morning he would send me a message of blessing and encouragement. This was a daily ritual for me when I would look forward to those biblical quotations from him to start my day. Inwardly I felt blessed by his words of encouragement. His words soon became vim for my soul that I longed for. I lived by them each day for encouragement and fearless will that Vincent's days of hopeless suffering would soon be history.

Then I began to find out who Vincent really was. He was a thirty-seven-year-old widower and single parent of an eight-year-old boy. Prior to his illness, he was an entrepreneurial, hardworking young man who defied all the odds in Ghana to become a successful businessman. His prosperous tile cement factory was well placed in the burgeoning construction sector of the Ghanaian economy. He was ready to be placed among the lucky few wealthy folks in Ghana who had risen from dust to the pinnacle of economic wealth.

Soon after the sudden demise of his wife four years prior, he noticed that his left eye was beginning to bulge out. He presented himself to a regional clinic in the hinterland but was referred to the eye clinic at Korle-Bu Teaching Hospital in Accra. Upon consultation, he was referred to the neurosurgical unit at the teaching hospital. There he was diagnosed as having a brain tumor after an MRI scan of his brain. This is where Vincent's suffering started.

The normal human instinct is that when we are ill, we present ourselves to a doctor and expect to get a diagnosis and a cure. But what is very frustrating to the patient is when the doctor says, "I know what it is, but I cannot help you." It is heartbreaking for us physicians to be presented with this scenario. Many of us have come across such a situation when we are limited and frustrated either because the treatment is too expensive for the patient or the condition is such that there is no cure for it.

It is too bad for the doctor facing such a conundrum. But being a patient facing such a scenario is even more devastating. This was the predicament Vincent found himself in when I came into his life. He had no money to cosmetically remove the brain tumor that was pushing his left eye out of its socket so was unable to determine whether the brain tumor was the curable type.

Korle-Bu Teaching Hospital in Ghana was the last bus stop for Vincent. It is the premium hospital in the country, but for all its glory, the medical school that trained me has lagged behind in technology. Its severe deficiency in modern technology became apparent when Vincent's neurosurgeon told him that he could operate on him in Ghana but that there was no intensive-care unit equipped well enough to tend to his postoperative needs.

His doctor suggested seeking treatment abroad. India became the obvious choice. This is because of their high quality medical care at a relatively affordable price. After Vincent made his own preliminary inquiry in India, he was given a price tag of $20,000 for his treatment.

For four years Vincent had been trying, unsuccessfully, to find money for the removal of his brain tumor. During this period, however, he had seen the tumor gradually grow in size, pushing his left eye out of its socket. He had suffered the agony of progressive loss of sight in that eye until it became totally blind.

Vincent lived in pain and suffering for four years. His left eyelid was unable to close to cover the eye even when he went to sleep. He lived through the nightmare of constant eyeball dryness and irritation. He became very desperate.

Out of desperation, he wrote an SOS letter to the former president of Ghana, Mr. Jerry John Rawlings. According to Vincent, the letter was intercepted by Mr. Rawlings's staff, who told him the former president's plate was already full. The only favor they could offer was to assist him in getting his story to the general public through the press. Mr. Rawlings's press secretary worked for Metro TV and was asked to take on the case to appeal for funding. And that was how Metro TV got involved in preparing the story.

According to Vincent and from what I gathered from Metro TV, the response to the appeal was very disappointing. An equivalent of $100 was raised. He used the money to purchase medication to control the pain in the affected eye.

And this was the point when I was contacted. I immediately embarked with due diligence to evaluate the extent of his problem and see if it was indeed treatable.

I sent him to my colleagues at Korle-Bu Teaching Hospital in Accra for an up-to-date medical evaluation. I forwarded the report to two different hospitals in India for their feedback on the prospect of treatment and prognosis. Their respective responses were favorable, which made championing Vincent's cause more palatable.

I also reached out to my colleagues in the radiotherapy department at Korle-Bu Teaching Hospital to see if they would be capable of performing radiation therapy if the need arose. They told me they would be willing and able.

To make the treatment affordable, I decided to split it into two sections. The surgery and postoperative care, which were beyond the capability of Ghana, were to be performed in India, and any follow-up radiotherapy could be performed in Ghana.

I have done much benevolent work around the world but always tagged to an organized group. This was the first time I stuck my neck out to personally provide a benevolent service to save a stranger's life. It was a responsibility out of compassion and a debut of my planned benevolent work. To Vincent, it was pure serendipity.

Up to this point, I did not have any registered charity organization. The fund-raising for this particular cause was purely based on my credibility and trustworthiness among my colleagues and friends. I encountered mixed reactions from many friends and acquaintances when I approached them for funding. It was a litmus test for me to distinguish my truly good friends from those who provided lip service. The few who rose to the occasion made it possible to come up with the money that covered Vincent's trip to India.

When that money had been raised and the surgery, which seemed hitherto impossible, was in sight, I decided to go to Ghana and meet Vincent for the first time. While in Ghana, I asked the Metro TV station to arrange the meeting. It was arranged for midmorning. I wanted to be there before Vincent, so I got there ahead of time. While I was talking to the TV crew, two people strolled into the room. We continued talking. Then my interlocutor suddenly paused and interjected, "By the way, this is your man."

I asked, "Which man?"

He responded, "Vincent."

I did not recognize him; neither could he recognize me at first. He wore dark glasses, so the eye protrusion was not apparent. I hugged him and had a long handshake with him. His demeanor was sober, as if to say, "At last my suffering is coming to an end soon." We were officially interviewed for the news of this important moment. For me, it was the big bang to launch my charity work, and for Vincent, it was the beginning of the end of his suffering.

After the interview, the TV crew asked that we go to see the ex-president, Jerry John Rawlings. It was his office that had presented the case to the TV station, so it was deemed proper that he be made aware of the situation.

The ex-president's office was a short ride from the TV station. It was obvious that he had been alerted to our visit. He was available and made time for us. The waiting area where he would receive us had a presidential air. The comfortable furniture, in light colors, was neatly arranged in an open rectangular fashion. The walls were adorned with pictures of the past glory of a young revolutionary soldier who risked his life to save a country infested with corruption and "kalabule," a term used to describe unconventional means to enrich oneself. Pictures speak a thousand words, and these rapidly reminded visitors that Mr. Rawlings did not become president out of greed but out of determination to save his motherland.

The sitting was by no means haphazard. Each of us was assigned a specific seat based on our purpose. Being at the center of the subject matter for which we were there, I was assigned the seat closest to Mr. Rawlings. When we were all seated, Mr. Rawlings was notified. As soon as he entered the room, we all stood to show our respect to a most revered and noble statesman.

We sat after he did. Then the TV crew introduced us one after the other. When it got to Vincent's turn, it was obvious that this was the first time Mr.

Rawlings had heard about his plight. The ensuing moments showed the other side of Mr. Rawlings that, like many, I had never known before and of which the general public has never been made aware. Mr. Rawlings summed it up in his own words in Ghanaian pidgin English: "You people go kill me paa." It literally means, "You people will kill me."

Mr. Rawlings sees himself as a great philanthropist who has selflessly spent thousands of dollars helping poor people in Ghana. This encompasses paying school fees, settling other people's hospital bills, and so on. He is unable to turn away from anyone who is in dire need of money to take care of a problem. When he saw Vincent, he was very heartfelt and deeply moved. His immediate thoughts were about how to help this guy. But he knew he did not have the funds immediately available. His words came out by reflex as someone who was frustrated at not being able to immediately help another person in dire need.

After a brief exchange with me, I told him I had raised most of the money already and that any contribution from him would be just fine. In deep thought, he scratched through his gray hair. When he came out of the apparent trance, he said, "I would love to offer you five thousand dollars, but I do not have this immediately available. But let me see what I can do. Tomorrow by eleven a.m., you will hear from me." The encounter, which lasted about half an hour, enlightened me as to the numerous benevolent works Mr. Rawlings has been engaged in since his retirement from the presidency.

At the end of the encounter, I thanked Mr. Rawlings for his kind gesture, and Vincent did the same, relieved that we now had more than enough money to make his treatment in India possible.

After a few days, the TV station presented me with $2,000 from Mr. Rawlings's office. This was unexpected, but it was more than enough to make a significant change in Vincent's life. His Excellency's magnanimous contribution was very much appreciated. After leaving Mr. Rawlings's office and with the cost of Vincent's treatment in India completely covered, I was ready to make the final arrangements to take Vincent to his next step.

In medicine, no treatment is 100 percent safe, and having the money did not guarantee medical success. I could not participate in the vibrant joy in Vincent's steps, but I held a cautious optimism until all was said and done.

Upon returning to the United States, I made all the necessary preparations for the trip. I arranged the airline tickets for him and his chaperone. I prepaid the hospital bill. I made available to him some pocket money for any unexpected eventualities in India.

On August 13, 2017, Vincent, together with his chaperone, boarded the plane for the trip that could potentially change his life one way or the other. The pictures he sent me from the plane spoke a thousand words. It was the first time I realized the significant role I played in his life. It was a moment that he had never thought would come six months prior. This moment, to me, was a junction of myriad breath-holding outcomes, and keeping a cool head about it was the only appropriate strategy.

While at Apollo Hospital in New Delhi, Vincent was thoroughly reevaluated by Dr. Rajendra Prasad and his team. He underwent further tests to ascertain the extent of his problem. All possible outcomes were clearly spelled out to him. This was the scariest moment for him. He contacted me from his hospital bed about the negative outcomes in the doctor's explanation. I told him the doctor was simply doing his job so there would be no surprises. All I could do at this time was keep the fear to myself and share with him the courage he needed. Vincent gave his informed consent, and surgery was scheduled for August 22, 2017.

For three days that ensued after the surgery date, I did not hear from Vincent. My world was quiet. I received a message from his chaperone that everything was fine. However, like a parent would worry about his children, I felt he was my full responsibility, whatever the outcome of the surgery, and waiting to hear from him personally created an honest and extreme anxiety.

Finally he sent me his postoperative video, and the joy I was looking for finally materialized. This was the time to celebrate, and when the pathology report confirmed that his brain cancer was a meningioma, it was even more of an icing on the cake.

If you are ever unfortunate enough to have brain cancer, pray that you have a meningioma. It is a cancer that is slow growing. It causes severe discomfort by displacing brain tissue, and in the case of Vincent, it was pushing his left eye out of its socket, making him lose sight in that eye. With early intervention, the prognosis is usually good. Vincent, however, had a late intervention that compromised the vision in the left eye. But he is blessed with the rest of his body, and I cannot underscore enough the gift of this quasi timely surgical intervention.

From his hospital bed, Vincent sent me a message that he was going to change his name on returning to Ghana. He wanted to add my last name to his and be henceforth known as Vincent Woode Awah. To go to this extent exhibited how sincerely thankful Vincent was for my help in changing his life forever. I am aware I gave him longevity, and a thank-you would have been enough. But I was deeply honored for him to take my family name.

My family name is not like the Joneses', Smiths', or Patels'. It is a royalty name unique only to my family. It is a nickname coined to honor the first king of the Shai tribe in the Greater Accra Region of Ghana. It means "the warrior who fought the British during their first incursion in Ghana to take advantage of its virgin richness." To be called Awah in Ghana means your origin is from the small town called Agomeda in the Shai district of Greater Accra. Vincent did not know this before deciding to be called Awah. He would soon realize the upscale recognition when his newly acquired name was in use. Vincent arrived back in Ghana a new man with complete resolution of his protruding left eye. No sooner did he arrive than he went to the high court to effect a change of name.

Vincent is proud enough to give me permission to present his image and documents before and after the literally life-changing surgery.

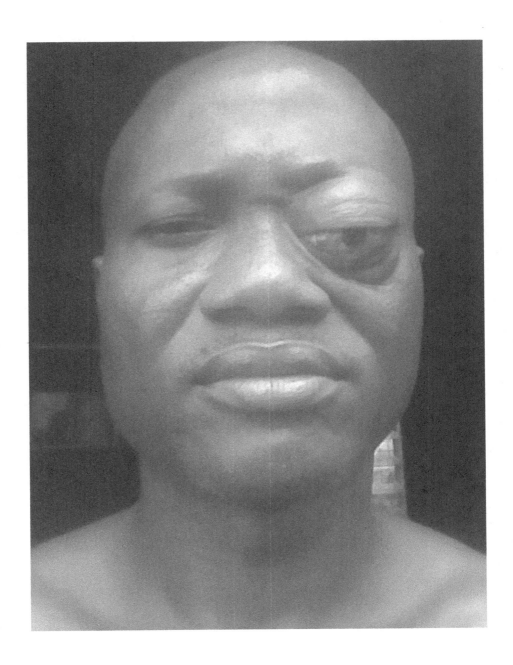

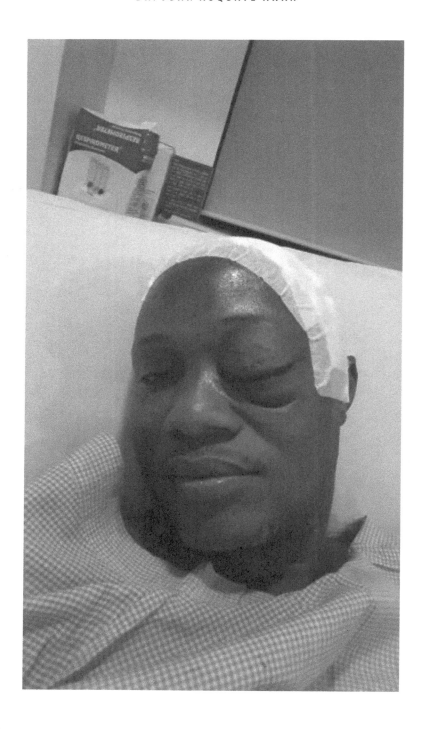

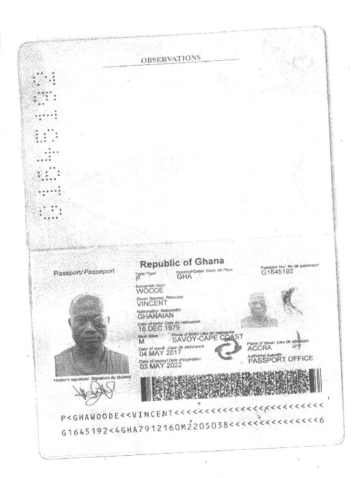

REPUBLIC OF GHANA
JUDICIAL SERVICE
P. O. BOX 119
ACCRA - GHANA

I, **RICHARD APIETU**, SECOND DEPUTY JUDICIAL SECRETARY OF THE JUDICIAL

SERVICE OF GHANA, DO HEREBY CERTIFY THAT **A. W. QUARTEY-PAPAFIO**

ESQUIRE, WHOSE STAMP, SIGNATURE AND SEAL APPEAR ON THE

STATUTORY DECLARATION BY **VINCENT WOODE**

CONFIRMING ADDITIONAL OF NAME TO HIS NAMES

DATED 6TH DAY OF SEPTEMBER, 2017 IS A NOTARY PUBLIC OF GHANA.

THIS ATTESTS TO THE STAMP, SIGNATURE AND SEAL OF THE NOTARY PUBLIC ONLY

AND NOT THE CONTENTS OF THE ATTACHED DOCUMENT.

GIVEN UNDER MY HAND AND THE SEAL OF THE

HIGH COURT OF JUSTICE THIS 6TH DAY OF

SEPTEMBER , IN THE YEAR OF OUR LORD

TWO THOUSAND AND SEVENTEEN [2017]

SECOND DEPUTY JUDICIAL SECRETARY

DR. JOHN ACQUAYE-AWAH

HIGH COURT OF JUSTICE
ACCRA GHANA A.D. 2017
IN THE MATTER OF STATUTORY DECLARATION ACT 389 OF 1971
AND
IN THE MATTER OF STATUTORY DECLARATION CONFIRMING ADDITIONAL NAME

I, VINCENT WOODE OF P. O. BOX AD 1204 CAPE COAST IN THE CENTRAL REGION OF THE REPUBLIC OF GHANA DO HEREBY SOLEMNLY AND SINCERELY DECLARE AS FOLLOWS:-

1. That I am the declarant herein and a Ghanaian by birth and nationality.
2. That I am known and called **VINCENT WOODE.**
3. That I wish to add **AWAH** to my name.
4. That due to same, I am now known as **VINCENT WOODE AWAH.**
5. That I make this declaration confirming my new name as **VINCENT WOODE AWAH.**
6. That I pray the authorities concerned to take note and amend records accordingly.

WHEREFORE, I make this solemn declaration conscientiously believing same facts to be true and correct in accordance with the Statutory Declaration Act 389 of 1971.

DECLARED AT ACCRA THIS   6   DAY OF)
SEPTEMBER, 2017.   )

....
DECLARANT

BEFORE ME

NOTARY PUBLIC
NOTARY PUBLIC
L. W. QUARTEY-PAPAFIO
P. O. BOX 3403
ACCRA-GHANA

190

I am proud to list the heroes and heroines who will forever be remembered for their kind and selfless gesture to save the life of a stranger they have never met and will never meet:

> His Excellency Jerry John Rawlings, ex-president, Republic of Ghana
> Dr. Prashant Patel, Chicago, USA
> Dr. Jisit Zaveri, Chicago, USA
> Dr. Seth Osafo, Chicago, USA
> Dr. Morufu Alausa, Chicago, USA
> Mr. Fritz Luz, Chicago, USA
> The Ghana-Chicago Club, Chicago, USA
> Dr. Christopher Chalokwu, Chicago, USA
> Mr. Davis Ferrera, Chicago, USA
> Mrs. Deneese Neequaye, Accra, Ghana
> Dr. Ajith Castilino, Chicago, USA
> Dr. Rudolph Kumaple, Chicago, USA
> Mrs. Leslene Kwame, London, UK
> Mrs. Georgiana Sedlacek, Chicago, USA
> Ms. Eva Stobiecki, Chicago, USA
> Dr. Michael Appiagyei, Chicago, USA
> Mr. Daniel Hawtree, Chicago, USA
> UGMS Class of 1988, Chicago, USA
> Mr. Tyrone Boswell, Chicago, USA

Vincent is now full of strength and vigor. He has discussed plans with me to restart the business he gave up when he was ill. I am working with him to make this happen.

The adventure with Vincent was nerve-racking but had a happy ending. It is a story that literally changed a man into a new man with a new name. He now walks with his chest out and is ever willing to also help less unfortunate strangers. To me, it is an inspiration to continue helping many more people like Vincent. It has set the scene for the philanthropic face of my mission on this earth.

While Vincent was in India for his surgery, my wife and I went to Ghana. We visited Challenging Heights. This is an organization that rescues children who work as slaves for their masters in the fishing industry on the Volta Lake in Ghana. The rescue is one piece of the puzzle in addressing the huge socio-economic injustice in the fabric of certain communities in Ghana. We will soon debut our new organization, Love to Be Me, to help the forgotten souls not only in Ghana but also across the world.

We are reminded our whole lives that others are indispensable. We depend on others for our upbringing, education, wealth, and so on. Without others, we would not be who we are today. If God asks me one day to name one good thing I have done for others so He can pardon me for my sins, I will say, "Go and ask Vincent." He is the "other" representing my big bang and the beginning of my philanthropic career.

CONCLUSION

Life is full of challenges. Navigating these challenges defines a person and shapes him or her into a certain form. The ability to deal with life's uncertainties is defined by many factors. These include one's genetic constitution, place of birth, family characteristics, parentage, and so forth. Successful navigation of these challenges depends on the strength of one's inherent burning fire, called zeal.

Zeal is a gift that can set you apart from your siblings, your friends, your spouse, and your community. It is the gift that determines whether you are a leader or a follower. It is the gift that makes you see the glass half-full rather than half-empty. It is the ultimate gift that enables you, no matter where you find yourself, to adapt and see opportunities rather than failures.

The village where I hail from was a perfect storm packed with all of life's challenges. There was extreme poverty, lack of education, beliefs that were antagonistic to human survival, lack of health care, and so on.

This microworld was packed with challenges, not unlike the tentacles of an octopus. No sooner had one gotten over one problem than another equally challenging impediment presented itself. It could be narrowly escaping the wrath of deadly diseases like malaria and tuberculosis to the inability of one's parents to afford basic education or provide decent clothing. Many of my contemporaries, even though they had zeal, were unfortunate and succumbed to the rigors of life prevailing in the village. The low life expectancy in the village of fifty-five to sixty-five years is testimony that the village life was rough and tough.

My dad lived in the village, and not only did he die in his nineties, but he also chalked up some business successes. He obviously possessed the survival gene and zeal. Since apples do not fall too far from the tree, it was not by chance that one or two of his progeny would rise from the ashes and carry on with the mantle of survival and success.

I appear to be fortunate to possess the legacy passed on by Dad—this zeal. It set me apart from all my family members. We were all presented with the same challenges on the same platform, but my deeds speak for themselves. Perhaps it was by design, and thank God it was so.

I was fortunate enough to be endowed with the gifts of intelligence, business acumen, and extreme compassion. These three virtues, intermingled with destiny, shaped the fortunes of my family and acquaintances. There have been many instances when apparent predicaments turned out to be blessings in disguise. I have many times questioned whether some of my successes were planned by divine intervention or serendipity.

Religious beliefs as currently practiced in Ghana and many African countries had many negative effects on my family, to the point where they created much animosity and division. This was the result of self-proclaimed prophets who used their so-called ability to see into the future of someone's life. They abused people's minds with information that was irrational but accepted as true by the victims. Such victims usually had little or no zeal of their own and always found someone else to blame for their shortcomings. The self-proclaimed prophets used psychological means to exploit their victims' weak points. They then took over their wits and used the fallen victims as puppets. I have experienced this firsthand multiple times, and it was not pleasant.

Notwithstanding all the expected drawbacks I have experienced in life, I have made significant contributions not only in the lives of individuals but also in my society at large. I delivered my family from the shadows of the wrath of village life to a city life that guarantees them a relatively higher standard of living, civilization, and longevity. I have given life back to total strangers who will outlive me and do the same for others. I am building a business empire that will guarantee jobs to people and help them become financially empowered. This will hopefully improve the quality of life for many people.

My philanthropic network has just begun, and it is always going to get better. I am giving back my excesses to humanity and the less fortunate so they do not have to go through the hardship I went through.

I would very much appreciate any comments the reader may have after reading this book. It will help me become a better writer for my future projects

Please direct comments to theamericandoctor2018@gmail.com.

ABOUT THE AUTHOR

John Acquaye-Awah, MD, CCD, graduated from the University of Ghana Medical School and the Royal College of Physicians in the United Kingdom. He was board certified by the American Board of Internal Medicine.

Acquaye-Awah has served as a faculty member at the University Hospital in Cardiff, Wales; Michael Reese Hospital, Chicago; Illinois Masonic Hospital, Chicago; and Mount Sinai Hospital, Chicago. He currently works as president, CEO, and attending physician at Dr. John Awah and Associates in Chicago, Illinois.

In addition to his medical and business careers, Acquaye-Awah is also deeply involved in philanthropic efforts. He has helped establish free health care for impoverished communities in the Philippines and Ghana.

In his spare time, Acquaye-Awah enjoys traveling, golfing, and indulging his entrepreneurial ambitions.